THE ONE WEEK WRITING WORKSHOP

7 DAYS TO SPARK, BOOST OR REVIVE YOUR NOVEL

KARIN ADAMS

AUTHOR IN YOUR CORNER

Published by Indigo Rose Corporation

25-1128 Henderson Hwy., Suite 198

Winnipeg, MB, R2G 3Z7, Canada

www.authorinyourcorner.com

www.karinadams.com

The One Week Writing Workshop / Karin Adams. —1st ed.

ISBN13: 978-1-896711-23-2 (print)

ISBN13: 978-1-896711-22-5 (ebook)

For Anita and Elenore

CONTENTS

Author's Notes   ix
How to Use this Book   xi

PART I
ICEBREAKERS

Hi! My name is _____, Writer.   3
Process Over Product   5
You Have a Gift (But It's Not What You Think)   7
Reconnect With Your Writer's Soul   9
Claim Your Writing Space   11

PART II
THE WORKSHOP

1. DAY ONE: IDEAS   15
The Art of Reading Like a Writer   17
Write With Your Eyes   19
Write With Your Ears   21
Big Box of Ideas   23
* The Inside/Outside World *   25
The Writer's Walk   29
Step Away and Get Active   31
Write the Back of the Book   33
Draft an Email to a Friend or Your Editor   35
Dwell Amongst the Books   37
2. DAY TWO: CHARACTER   39
Listing Potential Story Characters   41
Character From a Photo   43
Listing Character Traits   45
* The Character Web *   47
What Would 'You' Do?   53
Character Biography and Autobiography   55
The Journal Entry   57
Character Portrait and Action Shot   59
Assemble a Character Scrapbook Page   61
Allies, Rivals and Other Characters   63

3. DAY THREE: SETTING   65

    Get Sense-Sational   67

    The Picture Worth a Thousand Words   69

    One Space, Two Ways   71

    Scape, Scope and Scale of a Setting   73

    * The 5 Senses Web *   75

    Activate Your Story's World   79

    Make a Map   81

    Write a Brief History of Your World   83

    Build Your Story's World   85

    Visit Your Character's Bedroom   87

    Enlarge Your Story's World   89

4. DAY FOUR: PLOT AND PLANNING   91

    Storyboard Prep   93

    Step 1: Set Up Your Board   95

    Step 2: Goals/Problems   97

    Step 3: Anchor Your Plot at Both Ends   101

    Step 4: MIDDLE 1–Searching, Trying, and Obstacles   105

    Step 5: MIDDLE 2–Game Changers and Best Efforts   109

    Step 6: Curtains Open   113

    Step 7: Curtains Close   115

    Step 8: Does Your Character 'Level Up'?   117

5. DAY FIVE: DRAFTING   119

    How to Begin?   121

    Beginnings Can Be Choosy   123

    Start on Page 1, Page 10 or Page 95   125

    * The 500/500 Method *   127

    More Show, Less Tell   131

    Animal Action Words   133

    Take it to the Mirror   135

    Drop and Give Me 20 (Synonyms)   137

    Practice Point of View   139

    Get Tense   141

6. DAY SIX: REST   143

7. DAY SEVEN: REVISION   145

    Sit On Your Hands   147

    Find the Keepers   149

    * BIG to small *   151

    Take a Story Inventory   155

    'Reverse' Webs   157

Get Loud   159
Write Your Own "Reader's Report"   161
Write the Back of Your Book   163
How to Get Feedback - Part 1   165
How to Act On Feedback - Part 2   167

PART III
FROM WRITING WORKSHOP TO WRITING YOUR NOVEL

Expanding on Ideas   171
Expanding on Character   173
Expanding on Setting   175
Expanding on Plot and Planning   177
Expanding on Drafting   179
Expanding on Rest   181
Expanding on Revision   183
Some Last Thoughts: Don't Be Afraid to Zig Zag 185
A Brief Workshop Reflection   187
The Best Remedies For _____   189

Acknowledgments   193
About the Author   195
Also by Karin Adams   197

AUTHOR'S NOTES

YOU MAY BE STARTING your first novel, stuck in the middle of a draft or wanting to refresh a project that didn't quite turn out as you'd hoped. There are wonderful resources that can teach you about the craft and the business of writing: books that explore the intricacies of story structure and strategies for writing engaging plots, books full of creative prompts to prime your imagination, books on finding publishers and agents and much more. Something that most if not all these books will tell you about novel-writing: at some point, you are going to have to write (a lot).

My book will not change this fact. But what I'm offering is something that can make the blank page or blank screen a lot less intimidating. I'm sharing my personal novel-writing *method*, one that will help you to gain *momentum* and to keep *motivated* along the way. *Method*, *momentum* and *motivation* are what I believe you need whether you're starting from scratch, hopelessly stuck or deciding to get back to it.

The seven-step method you'll be learning during *The One Week Writing Workshop* is the one I developed for myself that led me to write five published novels. But more importantly for you—*I've spent over ten years teaching this method to others in multi-session workshops, from first grade students to Senior Citizens.* At every age and every stage, I've seen my approach help to draw out rich, imaginative stories even from the most reluctant of writers. And if you picked up this book, you're surely *not* a reluctant writer.

So, let's break down the writing process together and start building on your creative ideas. By the end of the week, you'll have a reliable method that can take you from the first sparks to the glorious finish and a toolkit to face the blocks that can keep us from writing (a lot).

HOW TO USE THIS BOOK

ONE WEEK SPENT AT a writing workshop is clearly *not* enough time to finish your novel. But it *is* enough time to learn and practice a complete novel-writing *method* from start to finish, one you'll turn to again and again. Plus, you'll be acquiring writing tips for sparking creativity, elevating the quality of your prose and busting through blocks.

How does this workshop actually work?

The One Week Writing Workshop is a practical, activity-centered handbook that guides you through my seven-step writing method. It's designed like a personal workshop that you're attending for the next seven days.

Each Workshop Day, you'll do a little bit of reading—but mostly you'll spend your time on fun and inspiring writing activities that acquaint you with my method. When the week is over, I'll guide you through a brief reflection process and offer some concrete thoughts on using what you've learned as you write your own novel.

What will I write about during the workshop?

You can go into this workshop absolutely fresh, with no preconceived story ideas whatsoever. In fact, this may be the very best way to experience my seven-step method from start to finish—beginning with that very first exciting spark of an original idea. However, you might be *really* eager to use elements (characters, settings) from your current novel-in-progress as you're learning the method. That works too—and I'll give you pointers on how best to use pre-existing ideas as we go along.

Do I have to do all of the activities in the book?

No, you don't (but yes, you can!). Each Workshop Day includes a few Warmups, one Core Activity (marked with *), and some Stretch activities. Here are some optional approaches, with time 'guesstimates' to help you choose:

- (2+ hours per day) Skim the Day's chapter and pick as many Warmups and Stretches as you wish. Do your chosen Warmups, then move on to the Core Activity, and end with the Stretches
- (~ 90 minutes per day) Do one Warmup, the Core Activity, and one Stretch
- (60 minutes or less per day) If you are really pressed for time, do only each Day's Core Activity.
- **Go at your own pace.** Spread out the activities over several weeks, a few weekends—whatever works for you! Just go in order: Day One, then Day Two (etc.). And on each day: first Warmups, then Core, then Stretches.

Don't worry about activities you might decide to skip during your workshop. After the workshop, this book becomes an activity resource you can refer to again and again as you write. I'll talk about how in the closing chapter of the book.

What supplies do I need?

You'll need: a notebook, a pen/pencil, some colored pencils or markers, a highlighter, and your computer.

Some activities call for a few extra items, like your favorite books, mini sticky notes, index cards, and simple crafting items (scissors, glue, old magazines). *Special Supplies* will be noted at the top of the page.

*A Word on Day Four (Plot and Planning):

I recommend setting aside a bit more time for Day Four. The reason is: on Day Four, I'm asking you to *do all the lessons in the chapter* and to do them *in order*.

On Day Four, I'll be walking you through the steps to create a mini storyboard. Each lesson builds upon (and depends upon) the previous lesson. You can think of Day Four as one big Core Activity broken up into an eight-step lesson.

In live workshops, this eight-step lesson takes about two hours, but you may want to linger even longer. (It's one of my most popular workshops—one that I think you're really going to enjoy!)

PART I

ICEBREAKERS

IN A TRADITIONAL WORKSHOP, icebreakers are short, snappy activities to help you get comfortable with your fellow workshop participants. In *The One Week Writing Workshop*, they are small but impactful concepts that may help you to break the ice with your own writing self.

Grab a tea or a coffee and read through the next few pages any time before beginning Day One. It's a chance to do some reflection on your current writing mindset—and possibly make a few helpful and positive adjustments.

Read these Icebreakers any time before starting the workshop activities for inspiration and helpful mental preparation.

HI! MY NAME IS _____, WRITER.

THE NAME THAT GOES in the blank space is yours. Copy this statement in your notebook and insert your name. Claim your identity as a writer this moment.

I mean *really* claim it.

Many of us who engage with the writing process and dream of writing a novel contend with fears and insecurities.

Will I ever finish?

Do I have what it takes?

What if I'm no good? (etc.)

Often, we have secret standards against which we are measuring our *right* to call ourselves writers:

When I write every day, then I'll be a writer.

When I write at least five pages a day, then I'll be a writer.

When I get through this workshop, then I'll be a writer.

When I keep an idea journal and use it daily, then I'll be a writer.

When I publish my first book, then I'll be a writer.

When publishing houses start calling **me**, *then I'll be a writer.*

You can certainly do or strive for any or all of these things as a writer. The trick is to start by affirming that you're a writer already and ditching the conditional 'then'. *When I write every day, then I'll be a writer* becomes *I'm a writer and I aim to write every day.* You see how it works?

For some, this little affirmation may turn out to be the most important step you take this week.

Now, you may have no qualms whatsoever about calling yourself a writer, no matter what stage of the process you are at in your creative work—and frankly that's fantastic. The point of this little prep talk is to remind you that *writing is indeed a process.* And more on this next...

PROCESS OVER PRODUCT

I F YOU DON'T ALREADY do so, I encourage you to start thinking about writing as *the process* you are engaging rather than the book (i.e., *the product*) you hope to produce.

Equating writing only with a completed product is risky. When you're writing a novel, the gap between the blank page or screen and the completed manuscript is incredibly wide. As you stare at that gap —or you begin to negotiate that great distance but keep looking up to see how far you still have to go—it's easy to get discouraged or derailed. Soon you're abandoning the whole journey. It's just too far away, too unreachable.

What if instead you choose to embrace writing as a *process*? First of all, you know that every process has steps, and of course there's always a first step. You've already taken at least one step by showing up to this workshop. That's encouraging.

Second, notice how we're thinking of steps, not gaps. Writing is a process with steps to take, not a huge canyon to leap across. That sounds more manageable. You can wrap your mind around smaller steps, learn them, and work at them. (This workshop is a great start.)

Third, even a difficult *step* is more approachable than one giant, impossible *leap*.

Fourth, while you may find certain steps difficult, you may deeply enjoy others.

By all means, enjoy the exciting dream of a finished book and of sharing the product of your process with others. But try not to continually measure your sense of success only against the finished product.

Process over product.

YOU HAVE A GIFT (BUT IT'S NOT WHAT YOU THINK)

H AVE YOU EVER GAZED at a row of books on a shelf and thought: *Wow, I wish I were gifted like these authors. I wish I had their talent.*

Or maybe you've received the following sorts of comments about your own writing: *You're such a gifted writer. You have a real knack for writing stories.*

I'm not saying that talent, genius, and knacks aren't real things. And I am NOT going to deny you the pleasure of praise and compliments when they come your way!

But I would like to offer this caution: when we connect words like *talented* and *gifted* to the craft of writing—or to any endeavor—we're often equating it with *something that comes easily*.

I don't know of any writer who talks about their work as something that always comes easily. But let's forget about doing a disservice to the efforts of the writers we admire—let's focus on the potential harm equating the ability to write with being talented or gifted can potentially do to *you*.

Some days, things are clicking. You're in the zone. Your writing is keeping pace with each of your most imaginative thoughts. I hope you've enjoyed such days and when you do—sure!—writing does

seem effortless and easy. But what about those days—or weeks—
when things are emphatically *not* clicking? When you'd rather be
doing anything else. When it takes an hour to write two good words if
you're lucky. Have you suddenly run out of talent? Have you just
discovered you don't have what it takes? Have you been a fraud all
along? Talk about a recipe for giving up!

What I'd like to propose is this: instead of thinking of the *ability to
write* as your gift, think of the *desire to write* as your gift. Do you see
how that changes things? *You have the desire to write.* Maybe you've
had it for a very long time. That's your gift. That's your fuel! And
because of this gift, you will learn, try, and explore the act of writing.

Suddenly, your good days and your hard days aren't measures of
your identity (i.e., a writer either with talent or without talent); they
are merely good days and hard days *for someone gifted with the desire to
write.*

RECONNECT WITH YOUR WRITER'S SOUL

TAKE A MOMENT TO remember the moment or time of life when you were first drawn to write stories. Does it mean going back to your childhood? Did you attend a reading by an engaging author? Could there be a place that captured your imagination, a powerful memory or impactful incident that called you to share a story? Maybe it was a particular book, book series or even a movie that woke up your writer's soul and made you say, "I want to do that!".

Now, take five minutes or so and write about this time in your life, whether it's recent or years ago. Describe the circumstances and surroundings. How did you feel? What actions did you take because of this desire?

If you want to go further, here's a further creative challenge: find an object, image, or tool—some physical thing—that reminds you of the time or moment you've just described. Grab that tattered book that ignited your love of story. Hunt down a photo of that inspirational place. Your grandmother always encouraged your writing; go find that colorful vase you inherited from her china cabinet that always makes you think of her.

If you no longer have the actual thing that comes to mind, can you represent it somehow? Sketch it out, or find a digital image of *a* forest if not *your* forest. Maybe you don't have the book that you read to rags as a kid, but you can make a colorful web that displays the names of the beloved characters and places in your favorite story.

Consider keeping this memento with you when you do this workshop or for the rest of your writing life if you wish. Let it help you connect to the time when it all began.

Remembering what drew us to writing in the first place can inspire us to keep at it.

CLAIM YOUR WRITING SPACE

SOME WRITERS HAVE AN entire room of their own that they can dedicate to their creative work. Others write wherever they happen to be with their laptop. Obviously, there is no one ideal writing space—and even if there was, we probably couldn't all have access to it.

Where do you do most of your writing? Scan it if you're there right now. Picture it if you're not. Conjure up the furniture and the objects in that room. What noises do you hear? What about the lighting? Feel the chair (or sofa cushion) under your body.

Now ask yourself—*is there anything in my writing space that makes me restless or distracts me from doing my creative work?* Clutter on your desk? Family members constantly walking by and chatting with you? Weird lighting?

I want you to take one tiny step toward claiming your writing space. I'm not talking about overhauling a space or banishing family and pets. I'm talking about doing one small thing that makes your writing space work better for you.

Here are some ideas:

- *Box up the clutter on your desk for the duration of this workshop.*
- *Grab a pillow and improve your chair's lumbar support.*
- *Close the door while you're writing.*
- *Turn off music.*
- *Turn on music.*

If you're happy with your space as is, can you think of a small, special way you might enhance it? Maybe you:

- *Change your screensaver to display an inspiring scene or phrase.*
- *Move the little plant from the bookcase behind you onto your desk.*
- *Designate a special mug to drink from whenever you're writing.*

Decluttering your desk or digging out a vintage desk lamp from the attic will not transform you into a bestselling author. Consider it an action you undertake for yourself—a sign that your writing and where you choose to do it is special and important.

PART II

THE WORKSHOP

You're about to get started on *The One Week Writing Workshop*. But in truth, you started the moment you decided to write—whether that moment was years ago, or today. You have a story (stories!) within you, and you've decided it's time to let it out.

We're about to explore all sorts of things together about story writing and the writer's craft. But this workshop isn't intended to teach you everything there is to know about story; *its purpose is to help you take action and bring out what is in you already*.

For each activity you choose to do, you'll read a little from me and then immediately *take action to create something*—all the while *learning a practical writing method* that you can use well beyond the pages of this book. So, in that spirit— let's get going!

1

DAY ONE: IDEAS

W HERE DO YOU GET your ideas? It's the question everyone asks a writer. And of course, the answer is that story inspiration can come from anywhere and everywhere and at any time.

But this doesn't mean that you should sit by and wait for a brilliant idea to simply show up. Today, we're going to practice the very *active* things you can do to *create the conditions* for creative inspiration, namely: observation, reflection, experimentation, and exploration.

Today, I highly recommend that you resist working with concepts, characters, settings, etc. from your current novel (don't worry—you'll have this option later!). I want you to experience how the following activities can help you spark exciting creative possibilities—from scratch.

THE ART OF READING LIKE A WRITER
WARMUP

Special supplies: a copy of a fiction book you've read and enjoyed before.

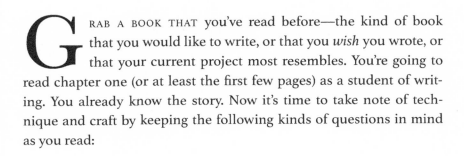

G RAB A BOOK THAT you've read before—the kind of book that you would like to write, or that you *wish* you wrote, or that your current project most resembles. You're going to read chapter one (or at least the first few pages) as a student of writing. You already know the story. Now it's time to take note of technique and craft by keeping the following kinds of questions in mind as you read:

- *How does the author begin the story—with dialogue, an image, an emotion, a mystery?*
- *How does the author convey information (personality, station in life, physical appearance) about the character(s). Is it through dialogue? Description? Action? All of these?*
- *What about mood and tone? What key words or phrases leap out at you that contribute to the atmosphere you are experiencing?*

- *Do you have an emotional reaction at any point in the chapter?*
  Why do you think this happened?

Make note of your responses and of anything else that grabs you about the effectiveness of the language, the cleverness of the plotting and staging of events. Jot down one or two techniques or approaches that you could imagine using to express a story of your own. Of course, you can continue on as far as you like in this book reading like a writer.

Two pieces of advice:

Please don't do this every time you read a book! Allow literary magic to do its thing and remain the delight in your life that I suspect it is.

Merely by reading (and reading and reading) you are a student of writing. You may not always be note-taking, but you are internalizing story structure, the artful use of language, plot devices, skillful characterization. So, just keep reading!

WRITE WITH YOUR EYES
WARMUP

Special Supplies: interesting photos from magazines, books, or online.

~

GATHER A COLLECTION OF interesting photos. Find them in magazines, coffee table books, or online—whatever sources you have on hand. Aim for about three to five images. Paintings work, too (or photographs of paintings). Images featuring people work well since they inherently suggest character and action. But feel free to use images *without* humans (nature photos, landscapes, architecture photographs), especially if you feel drawn to them. Avoid images of celebrities or well-known works of art as it might stifle your more imaginative responses.

The gathering process itself has already been guided by your unique creative energy; you've already made subconscious decisions about the sort of picture-story that appeals to you.

Now, simply look at your images in turn. Make observations and wonder along these lines:

- *What is happening in this picture?*

- *Where in the world is this happening?*
- *What happened just before this photo was snapped?*
- *What will happen next?*

If there are people in the picture:

- *How do they feel?*
- *What are their names?*
- *What are their connections to their surroundings?*
- *To one another?*

Choose the photo that speaks most insistently to you; maybe the one that resulted in your fullest responses. Write about the moment in that image. It can be a few descriptive sentences, a more developed scene or story moment, a poem—whatever you are moved to write.

WRITE WITH YOUR EARS

WARMUP

Special Supplies: two contrasting pieces of music (e.g., lively/subdued, light-hearted/dramatic)+ a way to play them.

WE TEND TO THINK of observation as something we do with our eyes, but our ears are also portals for inspiration. This creative exercise is a good way to train the connection between your ears and your inner vision.

Choose two pieces of music that you consider 'opposite' in terms of mood and tone. In my workshops, I like to pick one with a dreamy, moody, subdued feeling, and another with a lively, bouncy character. Avoid popular/familiar music as well as songs with lyrics where the words are likely to tell us what to see. Jazz, classical, symphonic, world, and even 'spa' music work really well.

Play the more subdued piece first. You can even dim the lights and lie down if you wish. Get comfortable, listen and let your mind drift.

When the piece is over, grab your notebook and play the tune again. This time write while you listen. What you write is up to you. It could be anything from a list of words that come to mind, a scene the music has prompted you to imagine, poetic phrases, or even original song lyrics. You might be moved to write about a memory or an emotion you find yourself experiencing. If you prefer to sketch rather than write, you can draw what you're picturing in your mind's eye.

When you're ready, do the same as above with the more 'lively' piece of music.

Afterward, reflect on both pieces of writing:

- *How do they compare and contrast both in terms of content, and possibly even in genre or subject matter (a poetic description in one case, an action-packed story moment in the other)?*
- *Did you feel compelled to connect the two pieces to each other in some way, make them part of the same story world?*
- *Did the music connect to a story that's already percolating within you?*

BIG BOX OF IDEAS

WARMUP

Special Supplies: a few random items from your space; a box or bag to put them in.

T HIS IS A CONCRETE, hands-on way to practice observing and wondering about what's right in front of you—actions that are often a catalyst for story inspiration.

Fill a box or bag with a handful of random items from your home. (Or, have a family member or friend do this for you to create surprise.) Pull out one of the objects. Look at it. Think about it. Then creatively muse over it in your notebook.

This musing can take several forms. You can invent a history and use (exotic or everyday) for the object. You can unleash your inner poet and simply describe it. You might choose to let the following sorts of questions guide your answers:

- *Describe the person this item belongs to. What's her name? How old is she? Where does she live?*
- *Where does this person keep the object? Describe that place.*

- *Where or under what circumstance was this object obtained?*
- *What would happen if this object went missing? Tell us about it.*

Pull out a second object and go through the same process as above. Describe it, connect it to a *who* and a *where*, explore the emotions it may elicit, and/or write about the actions or events you find yourself imagining.

Each object may inspire a distinct set of characters, settings, meanings or moods. Or, you may naturally begin to connect the objects to each other. Some writers might imaginatively transform an old-fashioned candy tin into a giant mausoleum imprisoning a dragon. Others might look at that same candy tin and imagine the reasons the elderly woman who owns it has kept this empty box in her kitchen pantry for the past fifty years. Notice the paths your writer's imagination travels when observing and wondering.

* THE INSIDE/OUTSIDE WORLD *
CORE ACTIVITY

I'M CONVINCED THAT THE best stories—even the most far out, fantastical of adventures—are rooted in something to which the author is personally connected. If your story is a genuine outgrowth of your emotions, memories, experiences, desires, or questions—that is, an outgrowth of *you*—then you are following that familiar maxim: *write what you know*.

Let's intentionally get in touch with a few things that have meaning to you. Write these three headings on a blank page leaving space below for brainstorming: **ACTIVITIES/EXPERIENCES**, **DREAMS** and **STORIES**. If you prefer to web your ideas, scatter the three headings over the page, each in their own bubble, with room to branch off your additional brainstorming work.

ACTIVITIES/EXPERIENCES: List a few things you like to do in your everyday life. They can be what others might consider a hobby (knitting, running, restoring furniture) or specific daily pleasures (sipping chamomile tea, soaking your feet, planning a vacation). Expand the list with activities you would like to do if only you had time, money, or a different life. What about activities you wish you had started in your youth?

DREAMS: What do you hope to one day do or accomplish? Is there a place you'd love to travel or a feat you'd like to master? Is there a person you long to see again or with whom you hope to reconcile? List a few dreams—fulfilled or unfulfilled—from your childhood. Feel free to *really* let your imagination rule the future: what would your life look like—what would the whole *world* look like?—if you could orchestrate it all?

STORIES: note the books, movies, plays, poems and personal/family stories that you love or in some ways have had an impact upon you. You can also note pivotal personal memories, moments in your life (happy, exciting, embarrassing, or painful) that you know have helped make you *you*.

Read over your lists. You might instantly see inspiration for a character's deep desire, for a moving story scene, or for a novel's theme. If not, let it percolate a bit. What did you learn, think about, or realize?

Activities/Experiences ✈

★ swimming
★ working as a department store elf
★ hot air balloons (Albuquerque)
★ board member

Dreams 💭

★ travel to Japan
★ own used bookstore
★ start after-school reading program
★ forgot to take an exam (actual dream/nightmare!)

Stories 📄

★ mysteries (cozy, magical elements)
★ school stories, humorous
★ Nana going to college at 75 (family story)
★ family cat returned after 8 years

stagehand for a musical

road trips

Activities & Experiences

camp counselor

half marathon training

follow a concert tour across the globe

house with the pond in the yard (recurring)

Dreams

write a children's series

Stories

fairy tale retellings

Tolstoy

when Uncle Greg ran away

THE WRITER'S WALK
STRETCH

Special Supplies: walking shoes and a place to stroll around.

～

WHEN I'M FIRST DEVELOPING a story, I go on a lot of walks. It's my time to let my imagination flow. I visualize potential story scenes like a movie in my mind. I allow dialogue to play like an audio track in my head. Sometimes what I see or feel or hear or smell outside—the slant of the shadows on the concrete, cool air on my skin, an irate crow, fresh cut grass—wiggles its way into that fledgling story. Specific phrases I roll around in my brain may find their way into my draft. Writing does not always require paper and pen or keyboard.

You're about to go out on a Writer's Walk on your own. Before you head out, choose an idea that the Core Activity or one of the other Day One activities may have sparked. This is what you'll contemplate on your walk. If you don't feel a connection to any of the ideas you've generated so far, get out there anyway. Simply pay attention to what you see, hear, feel, and smell as you stroll.

After meandering for as little or as long as you wish, return to your writing space and jot down your observations, thoughts, snippets of dialogue—whatever came to you or whatever you experienced on your walk. (If weather, time and space allow, have a notebook and pencil with you; find a place outside to note-take.)

In truth, I treat myself to a Writer's Walk at all points in the writing process, not just the beginning. (In fact, I just came back from one before revising this page!) I find that it's a great technique for shaking ideas loose when I'm stuck, and an opportunity to 'listen' to my characters who have a habit of telling me what to write when I return to my desk.

STEP AWAY AND GET ACTIVE
STRETCH

S OMETIMES WE GET COMPLETELY stuck. Maybe we have too many thoughts and ideas floating around in our brains. Or maybe none at all. Either way, it can be an overwhelming, paralyzing feeling. In extreme versions of this state, it's hard to do *anything* related to writing. And in these extreme cases, I suggest that you actually give in. Agree to temporarily step away. And don't do anything *related* to writing.

But—and this is crucial—this includes *not* ruminating at all about your writing. *Not* dwelling on your lack of production or direction. *Not* despairing about whether you will ever again be inspired. *Not* worrying whether you have what it takes to finish your book, get published, garner a loyal following, etc. Got it?

Of course, in this stuck state of mind, rumination is par for the course. And the only antidote I know is to do something completely different. Preferably, you choose something active—not necessarily a tennis match or a vigorous swim, but it could absolutely be these activities. Pull out a coloring book. Make a puzzle. Build a model. Play a board game with the family. Give the dog a bath. Declutter a closet.

In fact, what's worked best for me in frustrating times of 'nothing is coming to me!' is learning something new that also keeps my hands busy. During a particularly dismal dry spell, I remember buying some yarn in pretty colors, watching a half dozen video tutorials on 'arm knitting' and making several of those infinity scarves that were trendy at the time (or maybe they weren't—hardly matters!). The learning took my mind off ruminating about writing, and the knitting kept me doing something else. Eventually, my mood lifted, and I was ready to start writing again. I believe that in part, the creative satisfaction that came with making things—even though they were scarves and not stories—played a role.

So, when doing anything story-related seems impossible, do the impossible for a while.

That is, *something else.*

WRITE THE BACK OF THE BOOK

STRETCH

Special Supplies: a few fiction books.

❧

PULL FIVE FICTION BOOKS off your shelf and read what's on the back cover or dust jackets (wherever the story is summarized). Book summaries listed by online booksellers can work, too. *Really* notice what you read. What sort of details about the story are included? What's left out? What do you learn about the story you're about to read before cracking the first page (tone, theme, a crucial plot point, the central conflict)? What does the write-up make you wonder about?

Now it's your turn. Look over your notes for whatever workshop activities you've done up to this point. Grab the idea you played with that you feel most connected to. You may not love it or any of your ideas thus far—that's okay! Just pick the one that speaks loudest to you right now. If you only have a *who* (like that harried accountant or mermaid detective character you imagined), spend a few moments coming up with a *where*, *what*, *why* and maybe a few obstacles that your character will have to face.

If you've only done the Core Activity, mine it for inspiration. Let's say you wrote down "travel to Japan" in the DREAM category. Now simply add a fictional *who, what, when, where* and *why* around this idea and write the back of that book (the fictional *who* can of course be based on you).

Don't overthink this. Your write-up does not have to be earth shatteringly brilliant. It probably won't come close. The point is to get the juices flowing, to feel the excitement of sharing a story, and to help you discover something about the sort of stories *you* are drawn to write.

DRAFT AN EMAIL TO A FRIEND OR YOUR EDITOR

STRETCH

No, NOT TO SEND. And don't worry if you don't have an editor (yet!).

Review your notes from any of the previous activities. Pick the idea that you like the best of the bunch. Pretend that you've transformed this idea onto a completed manuscript or are eagerly developing this brilliant idea. Pretend also that you're eager to get some feedback from a friend with whom you can 'talk shop', or from your imaginary awesome editor.

You can summarize as much or as little of your imaginary manuscript or idea. You can be as casual or as formal as you wish. You can simply say *"Michelle—I've been playing with a great idea for my next novel! Here's what I have so far..."*. Maybe you share something about the tone and genre of your novel, and perhaps the intended audience. You can even include a bold statement about why exactly you think your story is fresh and unique. Have fun, show your enthusiasm, and sell it!

If you don't feel like improvising with one of your fledgling ideas, pitch a book you love, pretending for the moment that you are its author. (Why not? This is your fantasy!)

Don't worry if you feel a bit silly. We're playing here! I want to help you to keep connected with your dream that one day you will be telling a good friend or an editor (or an editor who has become a good friend) all about your dream project. Throughout this workshop, I'm asking you to focus on writing as a process. But it's fun to play with the later stages when you start sharing your ideas with others. Why not savor some of that feeling right now, at the beginning of your journey? It might provide a jolt of energy to help you keep going!

DWELL AMONGST THE BOOKS
STRETCH

Special Supplies: your library card.

❧

I F YOU'RE ANYTHING LIKE me, just being at the library stirs up a great desire to write. This might not speak to everyone who reads this book, but I bet many of you know exactly what I mean. Why not make the trip anyway? You could also head over to a local bookstore, preferably one that's always had that 'special magic' for you.

Here are some things that you can do at the library to deliberately stir the idea generation process:

- Find a table somewhere among the stacks. Do one of the Ideas activities from this chapter while surrounded by glorious books.
- Head to the section where you imagine your book will one day be shelved. Look at the titles. Touch the books your book would be nestled between. Get excited, and absorb the magic of this place.

- While you're absorbing book magic, grab a few books to take with you (please buy them if you're at a store!). Feel free to take a familiar title or author with you, but also challenge yourself to pick a title entirely at random. Have you ever done this? You might find treasure, or a new approach or style that inspires you. Even if your random choice is a complete bust, you can learn from that too.

- If you're not already there, head to the Children's Section. Search for a book or author that had an impact on you as a kid. Maybe it's the book that got you hooked on stories. Maybe it's a book about ocean facts that you read to rags during your *I'm-totally-obsessed-with-great-white-sharks* phase. Perhaps it's a picture book so vividly and beautifully done, you've always wanted to live within its pages. Reconnect with this treasure from your past.

2

DAY TWO: CHARACTER

I LIKE TO BEGIN with character when writing a novel. I make it my mission to get to know my main character inside and out as much as possible before I write my first draft. If I have vague notions about setting, plot and other story elements at this stage, working on character always brings these into sharper focus. If none of these other story elements are clear, working on character inevitably suggests story possibilities. After all, great stories flow from great characters.

Today's activities will help you to bring a fictional being with main character potential to life. By getting crystal clear on the *who*, I think you'll find it easier to later develop the *what*, *where* and *why*.

Remember: you can choose to create a completely new main character today for the purposes of The One Week Writing Workshop. It's great practice, even if you don't plan to 'use' him or her beyond this week. (But then again, who knows?)

Or: you can adapt the activities to further develop a character that you've created before. Just keep yourself open to creative possibilities and unexpected revelations!

LISTING POTENTIAL STORY CHARACTERS
WARMUP

W HO WOULD MAKE AN interesting main character for a potential story? You don't have to know what will happen in your story. All you need to think about right now is *who* you might enjoy writing about.

In your notebook, make a list of several potential story characters. You don't need proper names. Think more in terms of *competitive swimmer, fourth grade girl who loves science, 14th century Benedictine monk*.

To get the ideas flowing, remind yourself that characters can be inspired by things we love to do or learn about, by our own areas of expertise, or by what we one day hope to become (*dancer, hockey player, 21st century dad, archaeologist*). The notes you made for **Day One's Core Activity** can be a rich resource for inspiring potential character ideas.

Of course, you can open up your list to non-human and fantasy characters if you wish (*an abandoned lion cub, a shy robot, a dancing pickle, a warrior elf*).

Your characters can be inspired by those who populate the existing books and stories you love, but of course you'll always want

to be thinking about what makes your characters unique and
your own.

Once you feel you have a solid list, review it and highlight or
circle two or three that most intrigue you right now. Perhaps you'll
choose one of these characters for today's Core Activity.

CHARACTER FROM A PHOTO
WARMUP

Special supplies: magazines/flyers or online 'people' images.

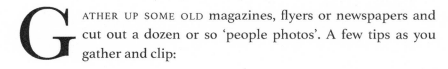

G ATHER UP SOME OLD magazines, flyers or newspapers and cut out a dozen or so 'people photos'. A few tips as you gather and clip:

- look for photos of people doing things—building something, cooking, conversing, reading a book, paddling a boat, climbing a mountain.
- avoid images of celebrities or well-known personalities (it may limit what you're able to imagine about them).
- include animal and/or 'fantasy' images if desired.
- (Optional) if you wish, glue the photos onto squares of construction paper or card stock to keep them sturdy and reusable.
- Adapt the above using stock photos found online.

Next, turn the photos face down, swish them around, and turn over five or so. Spread them out and just look at them for a while. Start asking yourself questions, such as: *What are the people in the photos doing? What are they like (friendly, serious, funny...)? Who do they remind me of?* Make notes in your notebook if it helps you think, or do the work in your brain.

After you've swept your gaze over the photos, zero in on the one that most piques your interest. For the moment, pretend that the person you tend to zero in on will be the inspiration for the main character of your potential story. Write down what you already imagine you know about them. Can you further develop any of these notes into a potential story idea involving this character?

Repeat the exercise with another set of photos, zeroing in on another potential 'main character'. Compare your two characters: Do they have anything in common? Are they wildly different? Which character do you connect with more? What did you learn about yourself as a writer in the sorts of ideas you came up with?

Were you disappointed that one of the photos you initially selected from the magazines wasn't chosen? If so—that character is calling you! Grab it now and repeat the exercise one more time.

LISTING CHARACTER TRAITS
WARMUP

CREATE A LIST OF the personality traits, attitudes/demeanors, and behaviors people display as they go about life and interact with the world. For inspiration, think of people you know, people you've read about (fictional/non-fictional), and even strangers you've seen interviewed on the 6 o'clock news. Your list might include words like: *bold, timid, lazy, clever, immature, impulsive, courageous, sensitive.*

Challenge yourself not to stop until you have at least a full page of traits, maybe even several columns. Dig as deep as you can: *passive-aggressive, overly demonstrative, reserved, easily-influenced, risk-averse, martyr complex.*

If you've done any of today's previous Warmup exercises, use the characters you've conjured up for inspiration. If you get stuck—or for a further challenge—look at the first few words you generated, then think in terms of their opposites. If you wrote *lazy,* add an opposite concept like *energetic* to your list. *Helpless/resourceful, bold/shy,* etc.

When you've finished, pick a fictional character that you created (ten years ago, last week, in the previous exercise—or on the spot right now). With a colored pencil or marker, highlight all the words on your page that seem to fit this person (or 17th century vampire).

Don't fear contradictions—*expect* them. Your character becomes more interesting and more authentic if s/he has traits that may (from the point of view of a dictionary) belong in different categories.

If your character seems one-dimensional and you want to introduce more texture, imagine some challenging situations. What situation would cause your otherwise *honest* character to act *slyly*? What circumstances would stir a generally *apathetic* character to take *energetic* action? What heights is your timid character capable of reaching? What obstacles might reduce your strong character to tears?

Pick a different character (one of your own, or a character from a book you know). Using a different-colored pencil, mark all the traits that best fit *this* character. Compare and contrast your characters. Do you see any overlap? What would these two people do if they found themselves in the same room having to solve the same problem? Roll your imagination over the possibilities.

* THE CHARACTER WEB *

CORE ACTIVITY

T HE BEST STORY CHARACTERS seem like living, breathing beings. Like ourselves and the people we know, they possess unique combinations of traits, cares, worries, experiences and dreams.

Sketch the following web template on a fresh page in your notebook. We're going to use it to help us create a multidimensional main character:

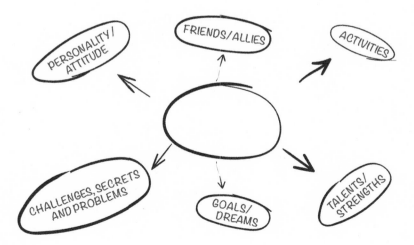

Next, take a moment to look through the work you did during yesterday's Core Activity (**The Inside/Outside World**) or during any of today's Warmups. You're on the hunt for an idea or two—something that intrigues you and that suggests a potential main story character. (You do *not* need to know what your story is going to be about just yet.) A proper name for your character might leap to mind, but don't worry if it doesn't. Character types, like *Bookstore Owner* or *Teenage Runaway*, work equally well at this stage.

Jot your chosen character in the web's blank center bubble. Then, for each bubble on the web, note one idea that connects to your new character.

I went through this process in the sample web that follows, inspired by the idea of 'swimming' sparked in my own Inside/Outside World brainstorming work. I decided to create a young competitive swimmer character named Mark:

After going around the web just one time, a picture of your character will likely begin to come into focus (like Mark the Swimmer in
my sample). Keep going, imagining this new character and adding to
your web. Start branching off more ideas from any of the bubbles—in
any order—as they occur to you. You might end up with ten ideas for
Goals/Dreams and only two for *Activities,* or vice versa. You can add
new categories if you want to: for example, new bubbles for *Family,*
Pets, Physical Appearance—even a catch-all *Other Facts* bubble.

Notice how Mark the Swimmer grows even more alive as I add to
my web:

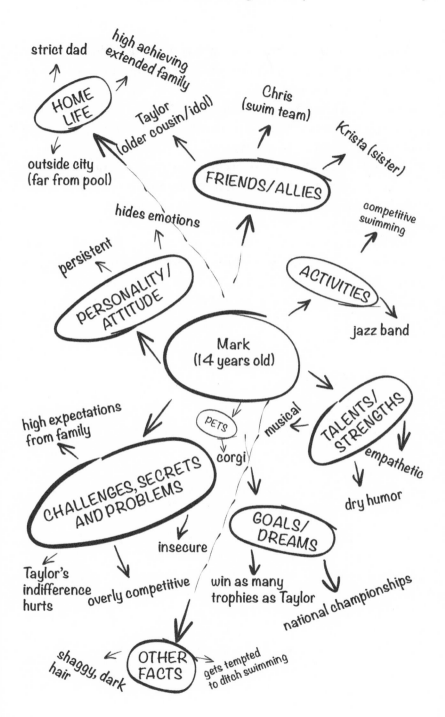

strict dad

high achieving
extended family

HOME
LIFE

outside city
(far from pool)

Taylor
(older cousin/idol)

Chris
(swim team)

Krista (sister)

FRIENDS/ALLIES

competitive
swimming

hides emotions

persistent

PERSONALITY/
ATTITUDE

ACTIVITIES

jazz band

Mark
(14 years old)

high expectations
from family

PETS

corgi

musical

TALENTS/
STRENGTHS

empathetic

CHALLENGES, SECRETS
AND PROBLEMS

dry humor

insecure

GOALS/
DREAMS

Taylor's
indifference
hurts

overly competitive

win as many
trophies as Taylor

national championships

shaggy, dark
hair

OTHER
FACTS

gets tempted
to ditch swimming

I find that the web format has a way of encouraging one idea to spark another (at least that's how my own brain works). It's like your character is waking up. Organic connections have a way of arising, linking the various ideas and categories. It's why I like using a web when mulling over a character rather than making a list. A web implies connection in its very structure.

When you've brainstormed as much as you wish, take a step back and appreciate your character. Recognize how he or she is quickly evolving from a mere notion into a much more complete person before your eyes.

We're going to build on this character in today's activities and in the coming days of the workshop. I wouldn't be surprised if your head is already filling with potential story ideas involving your web's hero!

WHAT WOULD 'YOU' DO?

STRETCH

Special Supplies: Scrap paper or ~ ten 3 x5 index cards.

G RAB TEN INDEX CARDS or cut some scrap paper into ten pieces. You're going to come up with ten questions to ask the main character you've begun to develop doing today's **Core Activity: Character Web.**

Below are questions I've used with writers of all ages. Feel free to use them, or model your own questions after them:

- *You realize that the special watch your grandfather gave to you has gone missing. What is the first thing you do?*
- *You are about to give a speech to two hundred people. What do you wear?*
- *Your best friend is about to move far away. Describe how you say goodbye to each other.*

Some guidelines as you create your questions:

- Don't worry about connecting your questions to a story plot. You'll simply be using these questions to get to know your character as a person, beyond the pages of any story.
- Try to avoid Yes/No questions. Aim for more open-ended inquiries (*Tell me about your grandmother* rather than *Was your grandmother kind?*)
- 'Desert island' questions work well (*If you could only bring five books, which would you bring?*)
- Ethical dilemmas can be revealing, too!

Write out your ten questions on the paper scraps or cards. Try not to pre-plan the answers. Turn the scraps over, swish them around, pick one and read it. Write out an answer in your journal *as though your character is the one responding, not you. Really* let her talk to you. *Practice* using his voice.

Remember that people don't always give direct answers—nor do they always tell the truth. They may evade, deflect or misdirect. Sometimes they tell you where to go. Or instead, they might offer a wordless, wise smile that speaks volumes. Ask your character your next question, and so forth. Notice what emerges about your character's voice, personality, and demeanor. How is s/he like and unlike you?

CHARACTER BIOGRAPHY AND AUTOBIOGRAPHY

STRETCH

W HEN YOU GET TO know your characters beyond the information about them revealed in your story, those characters will become more real to you. You'll find that it becomes easier to write about them; and ultimately, they will come across as more authentic to your readers, too.

One way to better get to know the main character you began developing with the Character Web is to write a brief Character Biography. Start by brainstorming a list of the kind of information you would encounter in a short, one-page biographical sketch. Remember that you can cover ground that may or may not be revealed in your actual story. Here are details that I expect would appear in most biographies—use it and add to it:

- Place of birth:
- Parents:
- Family members:
- Type of home/homelife details:
- Occupation:
- Daily Activities/Interests:
- Friends:

- Achievements/Contributions:
- Life-shaping experiences:

You can also come up with juicier prompts such as:

- Deepest secret:
- Proudest moment:
- Worst day:
- Biggest regret:

Using the prompts above, write a one-page biography for your main character. If you don't feel like writing full sentences, jot your answers beside the prompts in point form.

I've just asked you to write a *biography*, so you probably used the third person. What happens if you hand the pen over to your character and have him or her tackle the same information in a one-page, first-person *autobiography*? How does your character perceive and describe his own life, circumstances, her own self? Try it out!

THE JOURNAL ENTRY
STRETCH

YOU'RE GOING TO PRETEND that your main character is reflecting on an experience and writing about it in his or her journal. The topic for the entry does not have to connect in any way to a potential story plot.

For instance, you could choose a birthday celebration, a family gathering, a vacation day, or a day when your character felt at war with a friend—or the world. Depending on your character and your inclinations as a writer, you might choose to have your character use the journal entry to work through an emotional challenge or confront an old memory. Perhaps he or she is trying to capture and understand a provoking dream.

Once you've chosen your topic, it's time to channel your character and spend a few minutes journaling in his or her voice. Use the first person. Express yourself with language your character would use (even if *you* wouldn't). If you imagine a character with a cynical, dry sense of humor, let this comes through as she writes about her day. If he's methodical and detail-oriented, keep this in mind as you view a day in the life through his eyes.

Remember that a journal entry is not a report; it's personal and private. It might be a record of some event, but there's also room for emotion, opinion, and the deeply personal perspective of the journal writer. Knowing this, might your character be inclined to unleash snide remarks about others? Or perhaps reveal vulnerabilities that he or she usually hides from the world?

CHARACTER PORTRAIT AND ACTION SHOT

STRETCH

Special supplies: drawing paper and colored pencils.

~

MAYBE YOU LOVE TO draw. You might even be a skilled visual artist (those who write *and* draw—I salute you!). On the other hand, whenever you try to sketch the human form, it may look like a potato on toothpicks. No problem. This is simply a fun way for you to visualize elements of your story using a creative form other than words and text. You might be surprised at what shaking up the medium shakes loose in your imagination.

In your notebook or on drawing paper, sketch a portrait of the main character you developed with the Character Web. It can be face-only, or head-to-toe. 'Think big'—that is, use the whole page. This will give you room to zoom in and focus, to add details that give us visual clues about your character's personality like a wide, inviting grin or hair that droops over the eyes, hiding a shy soul from the world. Use color if you want—you can even break out the watercolor paint set if you're so inclined. And remember that clothing, hairstyles and accessories (bags, books, equipment, tools) help to convey information about a character's traits, life circumstances, and the time and place they are from.

Alternatively (or next), sketch your main character *doing something* —an action shot. The scene need not connect to any potential plot point; it can simply be a moment showing your character engaged in a favorite or common activity. Challenge yourself to include details that clue us in to the character's personality, habits and tendencies, hobbies, friends, and daily life.

ASSEMBLE A CHARACTER SCRAPBOOK PAGE

STRETCH

Special Supplies: drawing paper, a sheet of card stock or sturdy paper, glue, miscellaneous crafty/scrapbook items (buttons, pins, ribbons, tickets, etc.).

F EELING CRAFTY AND TACTILE? You're going to make a scrapbook page for the main character you've created—or rather, you're going to scrapbook *as* that character.

First, think about the purpose of a scrapbook and the types of things that people usually choose to put in it. It's more than just a photo album; it archives all sorts of special things (contest ribbons, ticket stubs, special letters and notes, that sugar-free cinnamon gum wrapper that reminds you of your first boyfriend). You might very well find a host of things in a scrapbook that has significance and value to its creator but to no one else.

Imagine what your character would include on a scrapbook page. Then go to town creating in whichever way you choose:

- You might simply *write a list* in your journal of five to ten

things we might find in your main character's personal
scrapbook.

- You can *sketch* five to ten imagined scrapbook items. You
  can draw the individual items or make a mock-up of an
  actual scrapbook page with everything laid out as your
  character would do it if making an actual album.
- You can *get tactile*: mine your craft space, recycling bin,
  junk drawer etc. and pick five to ten items that you think
  your character would include in a scrapbook. Think or
  write about why you (i.e., your character) made these
  choices.
- Go all out and *make an actual scrapbook page* using the
  intriguing crafty items you've selected. It may help to use
  sturdy paper and hot glue. (We're developing a multidimensional main character, so we might as well get '3-D'
  in our tactics!)

ALLIES, RIVALS AND OTHER CHARACTERS

STRETCH

S O FAR, YOU'VE FOCUSED on getting to know your main character. In doing this work, your mind may already be contemplating potential others in your main character's world: friends/allies, enemies/rivals, love interests, family members, etc. At the very least, you've probably added a potential Friend to your Character Web.

Let's coax one of these secondary characters to life. For reference, grab the Character Web you made for your main character. You're going to make a second web for one of your main character's friends. (If you wish, you could even develop your second character on the same web using a different color—a vivid way to visualize how two important characters compare, contrast and connect with one another.)

Proceed as follows:

- Write the name or 'character type' (e.g., Best Friend) of another important story character in the middle bubble.
- Go around the web one time just as you did for the main character, noting one idea for each category/bubble.

Notice as you go how your second character is both 'like' and 'unlike' the main character.

- Add more ideas for any of the bubbles.
- Add more bubbles if more 'character categories' occur to you. (If you do, consider adding these new categories to your main character's web as well and see what you come up with.)

Step back and appreciate the similarities and differences between your characters. How might their unique personalities shape the way they talk, act or react? What sorts of conflicts might arise between two such unique individuals?

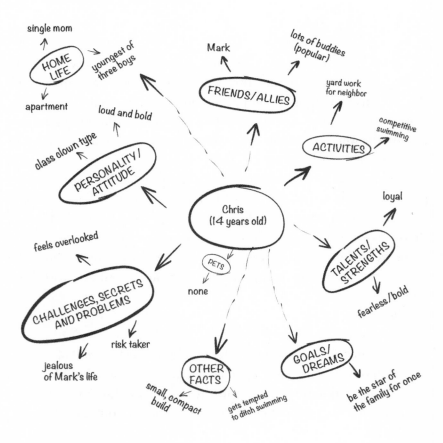

3

DAY THREE: SETTING

THE BEST STORIES MAKE you feel as though you've been drawn into the place where your characters dwell—where they struggle, strive, love and live. Once I've done some work establishing who my main character is as a person, I like to spend time in his or her world. The more I make this imaginary world real to me, the more I come to know that character, and the more I can write authentically about the experiences he or she will have in that world.

You'll find that today's activities aren't so much about writing long descriptions of your setting; they're about letting you, the writer, come to know your character's world inside and out.

The Warmup exercises will challenge you to write about places you haven't imagined before. When you reach today's Core Activity, you can continue working with places that are new to your imagination or further develop one that you've already been thinking about outside of this workshop. In either case, just keep your mind open to a sense of surprise and discovery!

GET SENSE-SATIONAL

WARMUP

THE WORLD AROUND US is constantly stimulating our senses. Stories can do the same thing. You know all about the five senses: SEE-HEAR-SMELL-TOUCH-TASTE. Let's take a moment to focus on each one of them right now, wherever you are.

First, take about 60 seconds and just look around. You can sweep your gaze over as many items as possible or focus closely on just one thing. When you're done, write about what you saw in your notebook. Pretend that you have this one chance to 'show' what you saw to someone who is not with you, using only words. If you had an emotional reaction to what you observed, can you write in a way that might evoke that, too?

Next, close your eyes and be perfectly quiet for another 30 to 60 seconds. When you open your eyes, write about what you heard. If you're in a quiet place, there was still something: *a whirring air conditioner, muffled voices on the television in the other room, the drone of an airplane in the distance...*

Next is touch. What are you touching right now, or what's touching you? Don't limit this to what your hands are experiencing. Describe the chair that's supporting your body, or the sensation of that nubby wool sweater against your skin.

How about taste and smell? If you're snacking right now or even anticipating lunch, perfect—describe it in great detail. Take a deep breath through your nose and try to capture your experience in words. Is there a dusty tickle at the back of your throat? Are the season's last lilacs just beyond your window leaving behind perfumed shadows? Or do you smell something less poetic?

You've just proven to yourself that to be in this world means to be experiencing it with all our bodily senses, even when you're just 'sitting there'. Remember this when you write. Using words and phrases that show how the characters in your book are experiencing their reality through their senses can help draw your readers into that same experience.

THE PICTURE WORTH A THOUSAND WORDS

WARMUP

Special supplies: landscape photos.

FIND A PHOTOGRAPH OR painting (in a book, magazine, or online) of a landscape or some kind of physical space. The image can include people, but it doesn't have to.

Muse over the following sorts of questions and capture your thoughts in your notebook:

- Does the image trigger any of your non-visual senses? Can you hear something, touch something, or smell something just by looking? If not, can you try? Write about what happens.
- Do you find yourself connecting to someone or something in the image more than the others? Is it central or off to the side? Is it hidden or hard to spot, but still significant to you? Is there something in the image that reminds you of something you did or once knew or once experienced? Write about these things.

- If there are people in the image, what emotions are they experiencing? How do you know this? Is it at odds what with the surroundings, or perfectly in sync? If it's a pure landscape or architectural shot, what do *you* feel when you look at the image? Describe these emotions.

Next, let's shift to imagining some plot-centered ideas. Write about what happened in the moments before this image was captured, and about what happens next. Who or what is about to step into the frame?

Can you imagine some dialogue between the people in the image? Maybe inner thoughts? Or is someone speaking 'off frame'? Write this down.

This exercise is a chance to explore a setting, and to notice how setting is much more than just a place and time; it's what we *feel* there. It's what *goes on* there or what *could* go on there. It's what it reminds us of. It's also a chance to explore your own perspective, state of mind, and what you feel drawn to notice and express.

ONE SPACE, TWO WAYS

WARMUP

FLEX YOUR SKILLS AT picturing settings and selecting words to
convey what you experience to your readers.

Write *"The house was old"* at the top of a page. Note down
what you instantly see in that old house. Don't stop at 'see'—what do
you hear, smell, touch or even taste? What about the emotions or
mood the place evokes? Perhaps your answers are along these lines:

- *Thick layers of dust*
- *Cobwebs hanging from the ceiling*
- *Broken windows*
- *Creaky floors*
- *Wind blowing through cracks in the walls*
- *Mice scurrying in the walls*
- *Shivers and gooseflesh*

Or...did you imagine a stately manor, freshly scrubbed and
polished for an upcoming charity gala? Or is your old house a cozy
World War II-era bungalow where your vivacious great aunt raised a
family, outlived a husband, and still lives to this day?

Whichever kind of 'old house' you first imagined, now imagine it's opposite—whatever that means to you—and write about it below the first one. Maybe this house includes:

- *A glittering crystal chandelier*
- *Shiny dishes laid out on a long table*
- *Thick purple carpet on a winding staircase*

Here are a few other setting pairs that you can experiment with:

- The forest in winter/The forest in summer.
- An elementary school/A high school.
- A luxury car lot/ A junk yard.

Spend a few moments bringing a few of these contrasting pairs— or any others you come up with—to life.

SCAPE, SCOPE AND SCALE OF A SETTING
WARMUP

BRAINSTORM SOME POSSIBILITIES FOR story settings. They do not need to connect to your main character at this point— this is just practice. Start big and focus in.

THINK **BIG**:
 Brainstorm a list of different landscapes. For example:

- Suburban neighborhood
- Desert
- Outer space
- Enchanted forest
- Large, busy city
- Seaside town

THINK SMALLER:
 Make another list. This time consider spaces on a smaller scale where a story could unfold. For example:

- Country Farm
- Middle Years school
- Hockey rink
- Dance studio
- A peasant village near an enchanted palace

This can be a fresh list with no connection to the first one. Or, you can make these smaller scale places branch off from one of your Think BIG ideas. E.g., *Suburban neighborhood*: *soccer fields, grocery store, Middle School, daycare center, new housing development, strip mall.*

THINK SMALLER STILL:

Take one of the smaller settings from your list, like a *Middle Years School*. Write down a list of specific items, activities, sights, sounds, and experiences that we might encounter there:

- *Middle Years School*: kids slamming lockers, overflowing recycling bins, pencils and lined paper, odor of burned muffins from the Food and Nutrition class, sneakers squeaking on a gymnasium floor.

* THE 5 SENSES WEB *
CORE ACTIVITY

BUILDING ON YESTERDAY'S **Character Web**, you're going to use another web to bring a story setting—or 'world'—to life. I call it The 5 Senses Web. Sketch a copy on a fresh page in your notebook:

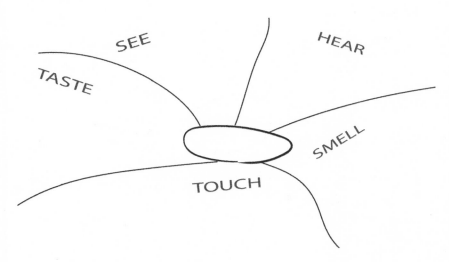

You're going to build a story world for the main character you created yesterday. Begin by asking yourself: *What particular place*

seems most connected to the main character I've been imagining? We're not trying to capture every location that would appear in a potential story but rather *a place with a deep connection to your character.* For my character Mark the Swimmer, a Swimming Pool seems right. For your character, perhaps it's a hardware store in a small mid-Western town circa 1987. If you're picturing an epic story setting, like a medieval kingdom, for now focus on a location *within* that world where you most clearly see your character spending time.

When you've settled on a specific place, write it down in the blank center bubble. Go around the web one time jotting down one idea for each of the five senses. What does your character SEE, HEAR, SMELL, TOUCH and TASTE in this world? Here is how I began to imagine Mark's Swimming Pool:

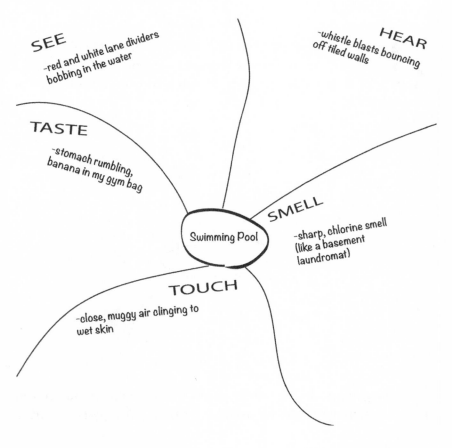

After you've worked your way one time around the web, more things to see, hear, touch, etc. are likely sparking in your mind. Jot them all down. Don't worry if you have more ideas for some categories than others.

Here is my completed 5 Senses Web for Mark's Swimming Pool. You can use it as a guide as you build your own character's world:

My goal was to bring the specific pool I was seeing in my mind to life—*Mark's* pool. Not all pools are alike: there are indoor pools and outdoor pools, Olympic-sized pools divided into lanes, and recreational pools with a shallow kiddie zone cluttered with pool noodles. I even found myself using the first person at times in my descriptions, like I myself was *becoming Mark* as I imagined the pool. After all, I spent Day Two getting to know this guy! This is *his* pool, the one he uses every day. It's where his friendships are made or broken; where he tests his edge every day, where he wins, loses and tries again.

Some of the details you imagine and note on your web may find their way into your story writing. Others won't. The point is for you to dwell in this imagined world for a while—making it real to *you*.

So—take your time and enjoy bringing to life a setting truly connected to your main character. We'll build on it in the Day Three activities that follow and in the coming workshop days.

ACTIVATE YOUR STORY'S WORLD
STRETCH

USING THE SETTING YOU mapped out with your 5 Senses Web, it's time to go exploring. But first, you need a mission —or rather, your main character does.

Take a moment to imagine an object from your character's world that, if it went missing, would rouse your main character to action. An object might instantly come to mind. If not, grab your **Character Web** to inspire ideas. Keep in mind that this object never has to actually appear in your story (and the little scene you are going to write never has to be used outside of this activity). This is simply an exercise for you to practice linking your character to his or her world through some action.

Now, get into your character's mind and body. How does s/he first learn that the item has gone missing? What about a first reaction— does she say something out loud? Does he feel sweat on his neck? Does she curse and kick the wall?

You've got the initial reaction. Where to next? Is your character flinging laundry about as he zips around the room? Is she on the phone, frantic, texting her friends for help? Is there a time for a deep-breath and a well-thought out plan, or do tires squeal as he leaps into his car and heads back to the office, or the pizza place?

Take a moment to write out this search, as though it's a story scene. You can write straight through to a resolution, or simply stop when you've had enough. The challenge is to bring your story world to life through the actions and reactions of your character who is motivated by a goal (finding the lost object). In so doing, you're practicing how you might incorporate your character's world into your writing without necessarily pausing to share three long paragraphs of detailed description about what we see, hear, and touch in that world. Instead, think about how the senses (the reader's, the main character's) are triggered *as* your character moves within it, gets stymied by its obstacles, and interacts with its elements.

MAKE A MAP
STRETCH

Special supplies: drawing paper, ruler, colored pencils (optional).

❧

OU'VE SEEN MAPS IN fictional works before, perhaps in books
you read as a child. Fantasy novels for all ages often include
maps of their epic and wondrous landscapes. If you have
one or two such 'books-with-maps' lying around, grab them for
inspiration.

You're going to make a map for your main character's world. You
can simply map the world you began to envision with your 5 Senses
Web, or you can go beyond it.

In fact, the world you chart can be vast in scope, encompassing
the four great elfin nations, the surrounding seas and oceans, and
jagged mountains passes to the north if your story leans that way. It
can be a contemporary neighborhood with houses, grocery stores, a
mall, and a skate park. Or, if you wish, focus on a single dwelling or
location you think will have the utmost impact on your story—a
home, a school, a skyscraper. If it's a building, consider making a
cross-section sketch that lets us peek inside all the rooms.

Whatever your world, challenge yourself to lay it out it in great detail.

- Grab a ruler and worry about scale—or not.
- Label key locations.
- Pull out colored pencils and make it pretty if you'd like.
- If relevant, use broken lines to indicate a journey.

This is *your* way of laying out the world of your story, getting a bird's-eye view of places and landmarks, establishing in your mind what your character knows (or will come to know) about his or her surroundings.

WRITE A BRIEF HISTORY OF YOUR WORLD

STRETCH

Y OU'VE MADE A WEB for your main character's world. Why not take a moment and write about it? Give this important place a bit of a fictional history.

How did this place come to be? How is it used and by whom? Is it a happy place, or was it once happy—until now? Are there any secrets, or ghosts roaming about (literal or metaphorical)?

Depending on the sort of world you're creating, you may want to acknowledge an epic history: a multitude of languages, lost races of magical creatures, a crisis that created the world's present dark conditions...

On the other hand, you may be writing a contemporary school story, but want to explore the flavor of the larger neighborhood—the sorts of jobs people in that community have, the cultural backgrounds of the neighborhood families, the reason for recent changes in the community's fortune (for better or worse).

Get further acquainted through your writing with the world that shapes your character, and that he or she may also help to shape.

BUILD YOUR STORY'S WORLD

STRETCH

Special supplies: crafty, 'diorama' supplies (e.g., shoebox, construction paper, paper towel tubes, colorful paper, fabric scraps, glue).

≈

OR THE CRAFTY-ORIENTED creatives out there—and those who like to think with their hands—send yourself back to art class or summer camp for an hour or so and *build* your story's world.

I've seen my workshop writers make dollhouse-sized homes for their imaginary characters and enchanted forests contained in shoe boxes. Others have made 3-D textured dwellings that pop off a page with doors that swing on hinges, windows that open, and cotton ball smoke puffs coming out of a chimney. You can go as far with this as you like. (Trust me, though — it's fun! This started as a classroom workshop activity inspired by similar things I saw teachers doing already. It was so inspiring, I've used it as a motivator for my own writing...and it works!)

Take a few minutes and grab crafty or ready-to-recycle materials: construction paper, cardboard, shoeboxes, paper towel tubes, scraps of cloth, popsicle sticks, colorful yarn, scissors, tape, glue. Give yourself some time to build your character's world. It can be inspired directly by the 5 Senses Web that you made, but it doesn't have to be his or her whole universe; you might choose to focus instead on a personal space or location.

Creating a model may spark story ideas about your character, or plot possibilities. Or, you might simply have fun as you think with your hands about your story. Fun is good! Fun keeps you connected to your story and can act as fuel to propel you forward when the writing gets tough.

You can spend a quick twenty minutes on this and move on.

Or...make it an ongoing project—a hands-on creative break when you're tired of writing or typing.

VISIT YOUR CHARACTER'S BEDROOM

STRETCH

IKE IT OR NOT, our personal spaces reveal a lot about us, and not just our choice in décor. Think about (or walk into) your bedroom right now and view it at as though for the first time. What kind of person lives here and what are the clues? Messy (*crumpled clothes on the floor*)? Meticulous (*sheets tucked with tight hospital corners*)? An avid reader (*stacks of library books piled on a night table*)? Devoted to family (*framed pictures everywhere, crib in the corner*)? Obsessed with getting away (*travel guides on the laundry basket*)? You get the picture.

Back at your notebook, take a walk in your mind straight into your character's bedroom or personal space (if your character is a tiny fairy, this could be a leaf under an enchanted mushroom—that's fine, of course!). Spend some time there looking around. Be really curious, even nosy. List what you see. Make notes about the sort of person you would infer lives there. What kind of feeling do you get while in this space? Messy places can be welcoming and cheerful; neat places can be oppressive or feel ominous—it depends on your character.

Now, based on your notes, write a paragraph or two describing your character's space. *But try your best to avoid using the factual, personality-type language that made it into your notes.* Let the space itself and the things within it offer up an impression of the one who lives there.

Consider this snippet describing an eccentric old wizard for a children's fantasy story. You could visit his bedroom and report what you see, like so:

The wizard was a very strange old man. He lived alone and enjoyed studying odd subjects.

Or instead, you could let the objects you describe reveal something about this wizard and his lifestyle:

The old man's hut sat apart from the others, beyond a crooked gate at the very edge of the village. Inside was one single room, stuffed like a Christmas goose with lizard bones, anemometers, and tattered books.

ENLARGE YOUR STORY'S WORLD
STRETCH

TAKE OUT YOUR 5 Senses Web for reference. Now, imagine a second important place that will likely appear in your story. (If you believe that everything will be contained within the setting you first developed, can you think of a place-within-the-place that you can explore in greater detail? A room within a building, for instance?) You can make an entirely new web for this second place. Or, you can choose a different color pen and write out your ideas for the second place on your first web using the new color.

If most of a teen-centered sports story happens at the swimming pool, perhaps some things will happen in a high school. If a survival tale takes place on a deserted island, perhaps your character will have vivid flashbacks of home.

As before, start by adding one idea for each category; then let your imagination loose using vivid, descriptive language to express the vision you have in your mind in words.

When you're done, step back and reflect upon the language you used to ignite the senses for both places. Do the two locations have distinct moods or vibes? Would you flop onto a couch and put your sneakered feet up in one, but in the other don your Sunday best and speak in hushed tones? Would your character stroll through the first location, and tiptoe around the second one? What would s/he be likely to do or say or what sorts of things would likely occur in each distinct place?

4

DAY FOUR: PLOT AND PLANNING

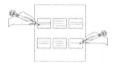

S OME WRITERS PREFER TO dive right into their first draft and see where the writing takes them. Others like to plan their entire story in great detail before drafting a story's first word. Whatever your writing profile, I'd like you to give my mini storyboard method a try. I like to think of it as a happy medium between the 'cold plunge' and working out every plot point and twist in advance.

Unlike the other workshops days, today I'm asking you to **do ALL the lessons in this chapter**, and to do them in order. Each lesson builds on the last as we create a storyboard step by step.

In a live, in-person workshop, this session takes about two hours. Some participants take more time for thinking and writing. **Be sure to give yourself enough time to go through all the steps in order.**

STORYBOARD SUPPLIES: a sturdy sheet of 8.5" x 11" paper (card stock is ideal), mini sticky notes (the ~ 2" x 2" size), and a ruler.

STORYBOARD PREP

M Y MINI STORYBOARD STRATEGY helps you to get a feel for your story start-to-finish before writing your first draft. It's not a place to work out every single scene and incident. Instead, you'll be musing over potential story springboards, key events and turning points. You'll be ordering these ideas on your board in a way that will help you construct a sturdy skeleton for your story.

The following steps will prompt you to come up with a story concept based on the main character and the setting you developed during this workshop. While you can use my mini storyboard to plan stories of any length—including your dream novel project—*if this is your first time through the workshop, please consider planning a short(er) 'sample' story to get comfortable with the technique and learn how all the components work together.*

Even if you are using a character and a setting from the novel that you've been imagining or writing for a while, you can choose to plan a smaller scale story 'adventure' for the purposes of this workshop. Remember that you'll be able to apply everything you practice today (and during this one short week!) to your own novel in short order.

Think of today as a practice flight that will make your real mission
that much smoother.

*The mini storyboard is one of my most popular 'live' workshops. I think it's
because it appeals to both planner-types and to those who tend to write
without a plan.*

*The planners get a tool that helps them to 'spec out' their story start-to-
finish—but it's not so elaborate that they never get around to writing (the
major pitfall of the planning personality!).*

*Those who prefer to just plunge in and write appreciate the simple,
straightforward approach of the mini storyboard. At the same time, they
have something they can refer to when they hit a sticking point in their
writing (and that's what's lacking when you don't do any pre-planning!).*

STEP 1: SET UP YOUR BOARD

Special supplies: a sheet of card stock or sturdy paper, mini sticky notes, a ruler.

⤳

G RAB A SHEET OF card stock, mini sticky notes, a ruler, and a pen or pencil. You'll also want to have your notebook handy for a place to record some brainstorming. Take out your **Character Web** and **5 Senses Web** for reference as well.

Using the storyboard image that follows as a guide, set up your storyboard including all the dividing lines, sections and headings as shown.

Over the course of the next several steps, we'll discuss each section—what goes in each one and why. You'll notice that we won't be filling in the board 'in order' (Beginning, Middle, End). That's because we'll be using the storyboard to focus on the *overall shape of our story* more than the order in which specific events occur. At every step, I'll prompt you to come up with a few creative ideas and then to fill in the appropriate portion of the board.

BEGINNING

Curtains Open   Goal / Problem

MIDDLE 1
(Obstacles, Problems, Searching)

MIDDLE 2

Game Changer   Best Effort   Outcome

END

Curtains Close

STEP 2: GOALS/PROBLEMS

I N MOST STORIES YOU'LL encounter, the story's main character is launched into action by a *goal* or a *problem*. There is something that he or she wants or needs, or a situation that must somehow be put right. That's where your plot is going to come from. Your character starts *doing things* and *reacting to events* in an attempt to attain a goal or solve a problem.

Some goals and problems may be overt and obvious (*to catch the killer, to find a way home*). Some may be more subtle, perhaps connected to the character's inner-world (*to grow up, to find meaning in tragedy*). Note that sometimes a character isn't even consciously aware of their own goals or problems.

You're going to come up with some possible goals and problems for your main character. Divide a fresh page in your notebook into three columns with the headings **CHARACTER**, **GOAL** and **PROBLEM**.

To get the juices flowing, think about a book you've recently read or that you know really well. Jot its main character down in the CHARACTER column. Did this character have a big, overarching goal? If so, write it under GOAL. Or, was this character faced with a big problem to solve? Write it under PROBLEM. Maybe you feel your character had *both* a big goal and a big problem. Maybe they're even connected to each other. This is common—write them both down!

If you wish, go through this process for a few other books that you know. Then, when you're finished, list the main character you created on Day Two in the CHARACTER column. Reading over your Character Web for inspiration, ask yourself: what *could* be a few goals or problems that would affect my particular character deeply enough to launch him or her into action? What would shake up their world— perhaps a goal related to work? A conflict with one of the Friends?

CHARACTER	GOAL	PROBLEM
MARK (swimmer, 14 yrs.)	-make Olympic team by age 18.	-pressure at home (grades? choice of friends?)
	-win gold at upcoming championships	
		-loss of love for the sport/identity crisis
	-switch from current team to more elite team	
		-unspoken competition with older cousin
	-quit swimming/devote self to jazz band	
		-rival on another team (saboteur?)

You may settle on a really compelling GOAL or PROBLEM instantly. If so, note it down—but then stretch yourself by brainstorming several more possibilities in each column. You might find a use for them later; maybe one will become a subplot to add texture and interest to your main story.

Still blank? Imagine that something (or someone) important to your character has gone missing. Finding that object or person can become your character's overarching goal.

Don't worry if you don't arrive at "brilliant" today! Aim instead to stay true to your character and to move forward building on your ideas. The possible goals and problems that I brainstormed on the sample notebook page suit the 'Mark' character I've created. They may or may not be brilliant, but they are enough to get me going on the storyboard exercise; I can build something from here. And that is the point of this step!

STEP 3: ANCHOR YOUR PLOT AT BOTH ENDS

L OOK OVER THE WORK you just did on potential goals and problems for your main character. Choose the one idea that most intrigues you or brainstorm a bit more until you're satisfied. Remember, *don't worry if this is not your most brilliant story idea of all time.* Focus on what you'll be learning by diving in and *practicing* the mini storyboard technique.

Once you've made your choice, grab a sticky note and simply write down this goal or problem. Writing in point form is fine. Stick this note under the GOAL/PROBLEM subheading on your board. We're putting it here in the BEGINNING section not because we necessarily will find out the goal/problem immediately on page one, but because a goal or problem launches your story into action. In terms of constructing our story skeleton, it stands to reason that the goal or problem will become evident in your story quite early on, near the BEGINNING.

Next, let's jump ahead. Take a moment and think about what will happen toward the end of your story with regards to your character's pursuit of the goal or problem—essentially, how will things 'turn out'? Write your thought on another note and stick it under OUTCOME. You do NOT have to know anything else about your story at this point. You're simply establishing what launches your character into action, and where this action ends up.

As you'll see on my sample storyboard, my character Mark's GOAL is to *Win gold at the swim championships*. My story's OUTCOME is simply *Wins gold*.

Of course, OUTCOME doesn't *need* to be a happy ending, nor does it need to be a direct fulfilment of the stated goal. Alternative OUTCOMES for Mark's story could be:

Wins silver medal.

Forfeits the race for cheating.

Wins gold as a coach but not as a swimmer.

In fact, I like this last idea better than my original OUTCOME. You'll see how I swapped out my first OUTCOME sticky note for a better one on the second sample board. This is why we're using sticky notes—feel free to do the same if your own ideas evolve as we go!

BEGINNING

Curtains Open   Goal / Problem

Win gold at
championships

MIDDLE 1
(Obstacles, Problems, Searching)

MIDDLE 2

Game Changer   Best Effort   Outcome

Wins gold.

END

Curtains Close

(with better OUTCOME)

BEGINNING

Curtains Open   Goal / Problem

Win gold at
championships

MIDDLE 1
(Obstacles, Problems, Searching)

MIDDLE 2

Game Changer   Best Effort   Outcome

Helps team win
as a coach.

END

Curtains Close

STEP 4: MIDDLE 1–SEARCHING, TRYING, AND OBSTACLES

THE MIDDLE IS THE heart of your story. So many things happen in the middle that I split the middle of my mini storyboard into two sections, MIDDLE 1 and MIDDLE 2. But it isn't merely quantity that makes the middle worth two sections. There's a certain kind of energy to the first half of the middle of a story, and another distinct energy in the second.

I like to think of MIDDLE 1 as the part of your story where your main character is beginning to engage with the goal or problem. The distinctive rhythm or flavor of MIDDLE 1 is thus one of *searching, reacting, learning,* and *struggling with obstacles* (internal or external). They won't resolve anything just yet, but they start to deal with the business arising from beginning their quest (i.e., going after the *goal* or facing the *problem*).

In your brain or in your notebook, brainstorm three or four scenarios that your main character might get involved in *en route* to the OUTCOME you've planned. Think in terms of *searching, trying, obstacles* and *tests of character.* (What might be learned? What conflicts might arise? What efforts will be expended? What bad decisions may be made?). When you're ready, write your three or four ideas on separate sticky notes, then add these notes to the MIDDLE 1 section in the order you expect these events to occur.

On the sample storyboard, I've shared my MIDDLE 1 ideas for my story. Note that there are triumphs and challenges, and that both test the limits of Mark's character—his competitive nature, his friendships, his desire to win, his goal to be the best, etc.

Remember that you can expect to make some changes to your board as you go, and maybe even more changes once you start drafting! The whole point of the storyboard is to get you started by offering a complete (possible) vision of your story start to finish. It might not be a perfect story blueprint just yet, and that's okay!

BEGINNING

Curtains Open   Goal / Problem

Win gold at championships

MIDDLE 1
(Obstacles, Problems, Searching)

Dominates team in a speed drill.

Accepts rematch with Chris – twist ankle.

Physio advises rest.

Mark persists Injury worsens – Mark is out.

MIDDLE 2

Game Changer   Best Effort   Outcome

Helps team win as a coach.

END

Curtains Close

Generally, story plots tend to move along with a sense of 'escalation' (conflicts deepen, obstacles became more impassable, etc.) But this does not mean that your character's journey through MIDDLE 1 needs to be a series of unmitigated and ever-growing disasters! Your character can have mini victories, resist temptations, and enjoy some fun and games in this part of the story, too. Forward and backward steps are allowed and help keep your story interesting.

STEP 5: MIDDLE 2–GAME CHANGERS AND BEST EFFORTS

I N MIDDLE 1, YOUR main character is *searching, reacting, learning,* and *struggling with obstacles*. But what if this twisty path to the destination never, ever straightens out? For one thing, you'll never reach that OUTCOME sticky note you stuck to your board. So, when you begin to plan MIDDLE 2, you need to start thinking of a *shift of energy*—away from obstacles, and toward clarity and resolution.

Cast your mind to the moment where things might begin to change in your story, where the momentum takes a significant turn toward the OUTCOME you've planned. What new information, realization or clue could pull your character from the muddle of MIDDLE 1 to the clarity of your story's planned OUTCOME? This is your story's GAME CHANGER moment. You can also think of it as an 'aha' moment, an 'epiphany', or a 'realization'. Brainstorm some possibilities and note your favorite on a sticky note under GAME CHANGER.

Next, on to BEST EFFORT. This is what your character does *because* of the GAME CHANGER moment. So, your character has an 'aha!', then *does something because of it*. In some stories, this could be the moment the hero realizes what she needs to do to conquer the villain. In other tales, it may be a bittersweet and emotional moment of letting go (of someone, of something). Brainstorm a few possibilities for these crucial MIDDLE 2 moments in your notebook. When you're ready, stick your idea under BEST EFFORT.

This is heady stuff. But I promise it's worth thinking about and will enrich your story. Take a look on the sample storyboard to see how I handled the GAME CHANGER and BEST EFFORT for my story about Mark.

BEGINNING

Curtains Open   Goal / Problem

Win gold at
championships

MIDDLE 1
(Obstacles, Problems, Searching)

Dominates team
in a speed drill.

Accepts rematch
with Chris –
twist ankle.

Physio advises
rest.

Mark persists
Injury worsens
–
Mark is out.

MIDDLE 2

Game Changer   Best Effort   Outcome

Sidelined. Sees
where Chris can
improve

Offers to help
Chris after
hours.

Helps team win
as a coach.

END

Curtains Close

The key to a compelling GAME CHANGER is to have it grow organically out of the plot. In my story, Mark has been sidelined against his will with an injury. But this sidelined position gives him a new, 'game changing' perspective on his swim team.

Similarly, the key to a compelling BEST EFFORT is to keep the character active. Because of his new perspective, Mark takes initiative and approaches Chris about coaching him for the upcoming meet.

Imagine how flat this same story would be if my GAME CHANGER came from outside the plot, like an unexpected snowstorm that cancelled the big meet. Sure, it could give Mark time to heal up and allow him to swim to victory, but it would hardly be a BEST EFFORT coming from Mark himself.

So, keep your GAME CHANGER connected to your plot and character, and make your BEST EFFORT a truly active effort.

STEP 6: CURTAINS OPEN

THE BEST STORIES HAVE our attention from the very first line —even the very first word. That's why I give the opening moment of a story prominent space on my mini storyboard. I call it *Curtains Open*, inspired by the curtains that part at the beginning of a play. As the curtains open on the set, a story world and its possibilities are suggested in an instant to the captive audience.

The CURTAINS OPEN moment I've planned for my story about Mark the swimmer is this: *It's 6 a.m.: Mark is the sole team member at the pool swimming laps.*

Now, instead of beginning with Mark waking up and having breakfast, packing his bag, getting nagged by his dad about his homework, getting into his mom's car for the drive to school—*splash!* we're right there in the pool. Not only that, without having to spend time reporting setup information to my readers, they will immediately and correctly infer that this is going to be a story about competitive swimming, and that Mark—doing laps at 6 a.m.—is one competitive, driven guy.

Take a moment to think about a scene that could open your story. Brainstorm on a separate page first if you wish. Is an aspiring dancer character twirling and sweating in a makeshift dance studio? Is a crime scene investigator snapping photos of a corpse? Is a corpse staring up at the crime scene investigator wryly promising to tell you about the circumstances of his recent demise? What scene, image or bit of action will hint at your character, your setting, the nature of your story's conflicts? (This is a great place to use your 5 Senses Web for inspiration!) When you settle on something that grabs you, jot it down and stick it under CURTAINS OPEN.

Note that the CURTAINS OPEN moment you're imagining may not involve your main character. You might be thinking of a scene that takes place in an entirely different place and time, but that hints at the story to come. Maybe you want to have a prologue, or to introduce a narrator who will tell us the main character's story. And remember that whatever you stick under *Curtains Open* can be changed at any time thanks to the wonderful removable nature of sticky notes.

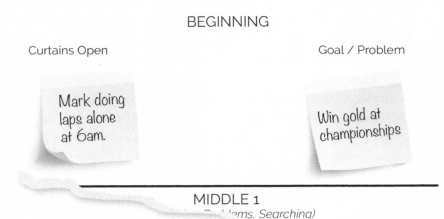

BEGINNING

Curtains Open   Goal / Problem

Mark doing laps alone at 6am.

Win gold at championships

MIDDLE 1
(Problems, Searching)

STEP 7: CURTAINS CLOSE

YOU'VE JUST IMAGINED YOUR CURTAINS OPEN moment—a potential first scene or moment that opens your story world up to your readers and draws them right in. Now let's jump to the very last section of our storyboard and the heading CURTAINS CLOSE. Continuing with the image of a play, cast your mind over the sorts of things that might happen right before the curtains draw together at the end of a live production. It could be a final bit of action, a strong image, or a poignant bit of dialogue—something that shows us what has been lost, gained, or changed because of the story we've just experienced. Perhaps it hints at what may happen next to the characters we've come to know.

On my sample storyboard, my CURTAINS CLOSE moment takes place some weeks after the big swim competition. Mark and his friend Chris—his former adversary—sign up together to help teach kids at swim camp. It's a simple moment, but it captures quite a lot: after overcoming obstacles and reaching his goal, Mark has grown from a pure competitor to a teacher and found common ground with his rival. This CURTAINS CLOSE moment suggests the shape of Mark's future beyond the book even though this moment in his life is the last my audience will read about.

What do you want to leave your readers thinking, feeling, or knowing just as they reach THE END? Do you want to show how your character became a better person, or how a relationship deepened? Of course, not all endings involve serenity and sunsets. Maybe your character is older, wiser, but more jaded about life. Maybe your character has lost everything. How can you show this change just before the curtains close? Or will you end your story with a twist or a cliffhanger to hook them for your upcoming sequel?

Brainstorm possibilities in your notebook. Jot down your best idea for a possible final scene for your workshop story. Stick it under CURTAINS CLOSE to complete your first mini storyboard.

Sidelined. See where Chris can improve

hou...

END

Curtains Close

Mark and Chris teach summer swim camp.

STEP 8: DOES YOUR CHARACTER 'LEVEL UP'?

THROUGH THE STRUGGLE WITH the central problem, or by striving toward a goal, your main character has likely experienced some sort of change by the story's end. He may be wiser, calmer, or more giving. She may have discovered something new about the world or herself. In some stories, a character may become hardened or grow disillusioned. This change may not be a desirable one, but it is still change. How about your character—who might he or she become by story's end? Or to put it another way, why did this story matter in his or her life (and why will it matter to your readers?).

As I plan and write I often ask myself: *With what foibles/traits/circumstances does my character begin the story? What does he or she decide to do because of who he or she is? What changes about her/him because of the journey?* Whether or not this change is good, bad, or indifferent depends on the character...and the reader.

Think about the main character in your workshop story. How might she change because of her experiences? Does he 'level up' in some way? Is he a little more of this, or she a little more of that? Grab a sticky note and write down how you think your character emerges as a 'new' person by story's end. (If you have a different colored sticky than the rest, use it for this special note.) Stick it on your board in the End section. (Add a Level Up heading if you wish.)

If you don't think your main character has grown/changed in any way at all, can you alter something on your board to make this happen? Maybe a new OUTCOME or GAME CHANGER would have a greater impact on your character's life. Don't force it—just entertain some possibilities! If you can't see a way to incorporate 'leveling up' into your storyboard right now that's okay! But keep the concept in the back of your mind as you write your draft.

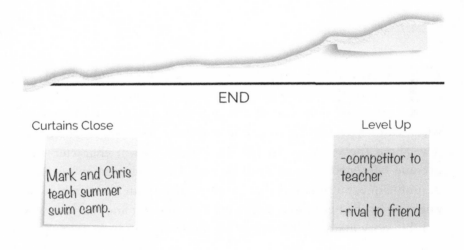

END

Curtains Close

Mark and Chris teach summer swim camp.

Level Up

-competitor to teacher

-rival to friend

5

DAY FIVE: DRAFTING

THERE COMES A TIME when you simply need to start writing your draft. No one heads to the bookstore to buy a Character Web. No one will checkout your mini storyboard from their library. But not only that—when you go from dreaming and planning with webs and boards to *writing a draft*, you're inviting a special creative alchemy to take place.

Grab your **mini storyboard**, have your **Character Web** and **5 Senses Web** handy, and keep yourself open to discovery and surprise. Now, let's get going on that first draft!

HOW TO BEGIN?

WARMUP

Special Supplies: three books from your bookshelf.

L ET'S LEARN ABOUT BEGINNINGS from some of the authors in our lives. Grab three novels off your bookshelf. You can be deliberate and choose three well-worn favorites. Or pick three books written in the genre you are most interested in. Alternatively, you can use the 'blindfold' method and grab three books you've never read.

Open the first book and read the first page or so. Then make some notes along the following lines:

- Note your visceral response—do you have any immediate opinions or feelings about the style, etc.?
- What have you learned already about character, setting, mood and tone, and the potential direction of the plot?
- Is there anything about the writing that you found particularly effective or impactful? Can you pinpoint a technique in use?

Go through the same process for the next two books. When you've finished with all three, compare your notes and thoughts.

Have you learned or seen anything that you might be interested in applying to the character, story world and mini storyboard concepts you've been developing over the past few days? If not, does this exercise suggest or affirm another approach entirely (one you may not have seen in these three books) when it comes to starting your own story?

If you're inspired, grab your storyboard from yesterday and draft a potential opening paragraph or two.

BEGINNINGS CAN BE CHOOSY
WARMUP

Special supplies: five or so books from your bookshelf.

❧

G RAB A STACK OF five or so novels off your shelf (if you did the previous activity, just add a few more books to the pile). Be indiscriminate. You're simply going to read the first sentence of Chapter One from each book.

As you read, notice and reflect on the specific devices or techniques used in each opening sentence. Does it use dialogue? A description? Action? A 'mystery'? An intriguing or shocking pronouncement? Make a short, point form list of the devices/techniques that you observe in these books. Chances are that among your pile of books, you'll see at least two distinctive ways to open a story.

Grab your mini storyboard and consult your 'Curtains Open' sticky note. For now, pretend that the idea you captured on this note will indeed be the scene that opens your story. Then, pick one of the story opener techniques you've identified in the list above. Draft a potential opening sentence using your Curtains Open idea, and this technique.

Now pick another story opener technique from your brainstorming list. Using this second technique, write an alternative opening sentence for the same scene. Once you've written the two sentences, take some time to reflect. Did one feel more natural to you than the other? Now that they're written, does one excite you more than the other?

If you're feeling *blah* about both sentences, or just want to try another approach—write a third (and fourth and fifth if you wish) opening sentence using other 'opener' techniques that you observed or that you know from your experience as a reader and writer.

Does one of the sentences you experimented with inspire you to keep writing? (If so, by all means...keep writing!)

START ON PAGE 1, PAGE 10 OR PAGE 95

WARMUP

W HEN IT COMES TO writing the first draft of a story, it seems quite natural to start your writing at the very beginning—the opening sentence of Chapter One. And sometimes you *do* hit upon that perfect opening line. The moment you've written it down you can't help but keep going. It launches you into a beautiful writing flow.

But other times, deciding how to start can leave you more blocked than ever. *Do I start with dialogue, or a description that will set the mood? Do I want to throw my readers into the action, or create suspense and hint at what's to come? First person or third person? Past or present tense?* Even though this is a draft, it's possible to get so caught up in these decisions that you're left more paralyzed than ever. And you haven't yet written a thing.

One way out is to experiment; try out several different openings until you settle on the one that works best for now. I've worked my way out of a few jams this way (hence the previous two Warmups!)

On the other hand, I've also succeeded in confusing myself further by over-experimenting. So, I'd like to remind you of this when it comes your workshop story or any of your dream writing projects: *you don't have to start at the beginning.* What a simple idea, right? But it's one that can save you a lot of grief, and something we writers often forget.

Instead of starting at the beginning, you can choose a scene from *any* point in your story—middle, near the end, even the very last scene of all. Maybe you can see a scene clearly in your mind, but you haven't a clue where it fits into your story. You can absolutely start there! Play out the scene in your mind, then transcribe it. Don't worry that it sits on your page without context. That will come. Sometimes writing out what is clear to you even if it isn't the opening scene—and even if you don't know where it will ultimately land in your draft—helps to get your writing flowing.

Let's experiment with this right now. Consult your **mini storyboard** and deliberately choose or imagine a non-beginning scene. Write a sentence or two of prose that would belong in that scene. Could you continue writing from here?

* THE 500/500 METHOD *
CORE ACTIVITY

YOU'RE AT THE DRAFTING step, the point where you're facing the blank page. In my experience, the key to breaking down its paralyzing power is to give yourself a daily writing goal. It should be *manageable*—something you can achieve on all but the most hectic days. It should also be *impactful*—so that you feel you've taken a step forward every time.

When it comes to writing novels, I've settled on the following drafting strategy which I've dubbed "The 500/500 Method". I write 500 new words of my draft each day, and I revise the previous day's 500 words. It's okay if my new words read like gobbledygook to an outsider. I can stop writing mid-sentence as long as my word count hits the 500-word mark. I am welcome to exceed 500 words. By revision, I'm not aiming for perfection, just cleaning up and clarifying language so that I leave things better than before. I can do my new words in the morning and revisions in the afternoon, or vice versa. As long as I find a way in the day to do my 500/500, I've succeeded.

After a few days of 500/500, I almost always get into a writing rhythm. I start looking forward to refining my previous day's work. Gradually my 'new word blurts' read less like babble—voice, tone, and style begin to shine through. I stop looking at the word count tracker and often exceed 500 words a day. And every day, the road to completion seems shorter. The other benefit? Because I've been doing a light revision all along, my completed first draft is more polished than if I'd simply powered through.

Your (modified) Core Activity is The 250/250 Method. Choose a scene from your **storyboard**. It can be the opening scene, but it does not have to be. On paper or on your computer, write 250 words of that scene. If your prose sounds more like a 'blurt' and is riddled with typos, that's okay.

When you've reached your word count, take a *minimum* 15-minute break. Don't touch (or think about) your draft! Then come back to your draft and polish it up a bit. Don't aim for perfect prose, just better-than-before. **Make a copy to mark up on Day Seven.** (If you wrote by hand, type it up and print it or take a picture and print it.)

1st Draft ("Blurt")

Mark shot out of the water a tht end of the pool gasping for air. The noise echoed off the high ceiling of the nearly empty pool. It was morning, dark and quiet.

He checked the time on his waterproof watch. It read a full three seconds better than the previous time. Not one to show off in front of others, he allowed himself a private mental fistpump. nNot that there was anyone there except the lifeguard. He reset his watch and prepared to try again. He dug into the water with his powerful breastroke.

Mark loved the water and having the pool to himself was one of the best things in the world. There was a moment when Mark slipped into the pool at first when it was cold, almost like it was telling him to get out, not go forward. A shock on the skin. But Mark had learned to love that feeling. He craved it like nothing else. When he pushed off the tile wale and took his first stroke, there was nowhere in the world he'd rather be.

He was in the zone now – that first leap ino the pool behind him. Now the sounds of the outside world had fully disappeared. TO mark it was the sound of focus. Nothing else mattered but Mark's determined push to be faster, forward.

It was over after a few more laps. The lifeguard blew his whistle. The old folks were lining up near the ladder, ready for their early morning water aerobics class. IT was no longer Mark's world.

Mark shot out of the water at the end of the pool gasping for air. His splash echoed through the nearly empty space, bouncing off the high ceiling. The cold light of morning was just breaking through the floor to ceiling glass on the east side of the pool.

Mark checked the time on his waterproof watch. Not bad. He'd beaten his best time by a full two seconds. He reset his watch and prepared to try again. He dug into the water with his powerful breaststroke.

There was always a moment when Mark would first enter the water. There was a moment when Mark slipped into the pool at first when it was too cold, almost like it was telling him to get out, not to go forward. A shock to the system. But Mark had learned to love that feeling, like waking up on Christmas morning. But when he pushed off the tile wall and took his first stroke, there was nowhere in the world he'd rather be.

He was in the zone now – that first leap into the pool behind him. Now the sounds of the outside world had fully disappeared, and everything became muffled. But it wasn't really muffled, it was the sound of being absolutely alone and focused. Nothing else mattered but Mark's determined push to be faster, forward.

After a few more laps, the lifeguard blows his whistle. The senior citizens water aerobics class was about to begin. It was time to get out. Mark pulled himself from the pool, the blast of air somehow worse than the first plunge, more foreign. The pool was where he was born to be.

MORE SHOW, LESS TELL
STRETCH

YOU'VE PROBABLY HEARD THIS advice when it comes to creative writing: *Show, don't tell.* Basically, it means that when you write fiction, don't think of it as reporting a series of events (i.e., *telling* your reader things). Rather, think instead that you are trying to draw your reader into the very experience of your story—what it looks like, sounds like and feels like to be there. This is *showing* your story. When readers are shown a story, they are more likely to connect, emotionally and otherwise, to what's going on in our tale.

Imagine if the following sentence appeared in my story about Mark the swimmer: *Mark was sad.* I am *telling* you that my character, Mark was sad.

But if instead I wrote *Mark cried*, I've started to paint you a picture. *Mark kicked the wall on his way out of the room* could also work. How about *Mark turned his face away as a hot tear threatened to roll down his cheek.* Notice the difference? Instead of telling you about Mark's emotional state, I'm showing you the way his sadness unfolds.

It's important to note that 'showing' isn't necessarily about writing more words, using more adjectives, or inserting clever metaphors. It's not at all about using a greater *quantity* of words and details, but crafting sentences with greater *impact*.

In your notebook, practice turning the following 'tells' into 'shows'. You can use dialogue, gestures, and settings to show us more about the characters and what is going on in these 'story moments', and feel free to write more than a sentence for each idea if you wish:

- *Sara was extremely organized.*
- *The brothers argued over who should go first.*
- *The house was old.*
- *The couple was running out of time.*

As you can see from the title I've given to this activity, I like to modify the well-known rule *Show, don't tell* to *More show, less tell.* Sometimes a direct statement of fact—a *tell*—is *exactly* what a given moment in your story needs! I prefer to think that we should *strive* to do *more showing* in our writing than telling, but that at certain times telling is a valid option.

ANIMAL ACTION WORDS

STRETCH

S OMETIMES WHEN WE'RE IN the thick of drafting, we lose sight of the fun we're supposed to be having with words. Especially when those words aren't flowing. Forget 'fun'—in those moments, words seem like *the enemy*. Let's take a few minutes right now to lighten up!

Divide a fresh page into two columns. Write the word WENT as the heading for the first column and SAID as the heading for the second.

Now, tell me this: what would you say if I asked you how a snake moves from Point A to Point B? You'd probably say it would *slither*. Write the word *slithered* in the WENT column. What about a duck? Ducks 'waddle', right? Add *waddled* to this same list.

Get out a timer and set it for sixty seconds. You have one minute to list as many different verbs you can think of that capture how animals move (*lumbered*, *skittered*, *flew* etc.). Remember that animals 'move' in the forest, sky, water, and desert, too. 3,2,1...*GO!*

When your time is up, admire your list. How many words did you come up with?

Now, move on to the SAID column. You're going to come up with words that you might use if an animal were to speak in a story (e.g., snake = *hissed*; bear = *growled*; fish = *burped*). Set another minute on your timer. 3,2,1...*GO!*

How did you do this time? Did you unleash any words that were particularly delightful to you? Could you use any of the words from these two lists in the draft writing piece you did for the Core Activity? Even if your story is populated with humans, maybe someone *hisses* when they speak, or *stomps* from the room in anger...

I use this activity in my live workshops as a whimsical break. It helps remind us writers that words are a pleasure—and also to show you how many words can pour out of you when you focus. I'll bet your lists are quite impressive for something you weren't planning to do two minutes ago! Are there other ways in your life that you can connect with the joy of words? Crossword puzzles? Word searches? Magnet poetry on the fridge? When words seem to be your enemy, be the bigger person and invite them over to play.

TAKE IT TO THE MIRROR
STRETCH

Special supplies: access to a room with a mirror.

❧

WHEN I'M HAVING A particularly intense writing session, I find myself mumbling bits of dialogue out loud, or gesturing the way my character might. Does this ever happen to you? For me, it's the feeling of the story really coming alive; in those moments I'm literally *embodying* the action I'm creating. It's a pretty sweet feeling—definitely a part of that 'flow' we're always looking for as writers.

Sometimes all this muttering and miming inspires the actual words I write down to capture my character's tone of voice as she bares her soul, or the sensations that ripple through his body as he shapes his hand into a fist under the table.

Not every writing session results in this mystical communion between a writer's mind, body and keyboard. But sometimes you can conjure up this experience by leaving your desk and hanging out in front of a mirror. Once you're there, step into your character's body and act out the story moment that has you stumped. You might even become two characters at once, dramatizing a conversation. Listen to your own voice as you improvise dialogue. Watch as emotions and physical sensations bubble to the surface and show themselves in gestures, twitches, twists and turns. Take note of what all this looks like, sounds like, feels like.

Why don't you try this now? Scan your written piece from today's Core Activity. Is there a moment you could take to the mirror for a bit of impromptu Drama 101? Spend a few minutes 'acting out' your story scene in front of a mirror (you may want to close the door!). Something you utter out loud may inspire a great bit of dialogue. Or, what you observe about your own body language may inspire description that will add color to a scene.

Go back to your written piece. What might you now add or alter after hanging out with your mirror? Make notes or changes as you see fit.

DROP AND GIVE ME 20 (SYNONYMS)
STRETCH

H AVE YOU EVER BEEN called out for overusing a word? I have. The first time was when my fourth grade teacher pointed out that I overused the word 'nice' in my writing. She advised me to buy a thesaurus. My mother took me to the bookstore that very night, and I've been using wonderful, splendid, refined and dazzling new words ever since. (And yes, you can overuse your thesaurus.)

Ever since the NICE incident, the thrill of hitting upon just the right word has never left me. I learned that writing was about much more than coming up with exciting ideas; the words you choose to express those ideas count, too. It also suggested what revision could do to a story. You could look back over your work and swap your first words for better ones, bringing your story more vividly to life.

You're going to exercise your own inner thesaurus. Divide a notebook page into two sections and write the word NICE (humor me!) as a heading for one of the sections. Right now, without any further thought, write a list of at least twenty synonyms for NICE.

How did that go?

Now write the word SCARED as the heading for the second

section. Once more, 'drop and give me twenty' different words that you might use in place of SCARED.

When you're done, spend a bit of time examining your lists. Notice that even though you've listed synonyms, not every word on your list is interchangeable in a strict sense. You might say *Have a nice day* but probably never *Have a satisfactory day*. Similarly, *Sam was petrified as the roller coaster reached the top* sounds right, while *Sam was intimidated as the roller coaster reached the top* does not (even though *petrified* and *intimidated* are both legitimate synonyms for scared). Likewise, words like *splendid* and *affrighted* may have made your list, but they're more likely to find a home in your historical fiction novel than in your contemporary middle school story (*epic* and *freaked out* might work better there).

Context and tone matter. And finding just the right word to let you express yourself is part of the joy of writing. Something to savor as you continue drafting!

PRACTICE POINT OF VIEW
STRETCH

I WROTE THE FIRST draft of my first published novel (*Lights! Curtains! Cows!*) in third person narration ("he/she/they" story-telling). Upon re-reading, something about it felt 'off'. The humorous story I envisioned in my mind was falling flat. On a whim, I wondered what would happen if I switched to the first person ("I" storytelling) and had my bold female protagonist narrate the story. That didn't work either. Heading back to the drawing board once more, this time I put the story in the mouth of my protagonist's hapless best friend. Suddenly I had a relatable narrator with a reluctant, cynical, *here-we-go-again* voice that was spot on for my particular story.

The point of this little anecdote is that choosing the right narrative voice and the right set of eyes through which to recount your tale is an important drafting consideration. So, here's your task: Pick a paragraph from the writing you did for the Core Activity (the lightly revised version). If you initially used the first person, rewrite this moment using the third person (and if you used third, now use first). You can even experiment further and let a different character from your story recount this same scene in the first person.

Do some reflection on your little experiment. Does one point of view feel like a more natural fit for your story? (You may have to do a bit more writing to really find out, but you can check in with your gut even now.) Were you pleasantly surprised when you switched 'persons', or did this just affirm that you made the right choice in the first place? Which point of view offered the most freedom in how you could represent the scene? Do any other storytelling advantages occur to you? Which version makes you want to keep writing?

Of course, as you probably know, there are many choices available beyond simply 'third or first person'. (Remember terms like 'limited' and 'omniscient'? What about stories with multiple narrators and viewpoints? You have lots of options!) If this inspires another narrative approach, experiment with it a bit right now.

GET TENSE

STRETCH

I T'S PROBABLY SAFE TO say that the majority of stories are written in the past tense:

> *Mark headed for the edge of the pool. Ignoring the lifeguard's whistle, he plunged in...*

Of course, some are written in the present tense:

> *Mark heads for the edge of the pool. He ignores the lifeguard's whistle. He plunges in...*

Different tenses can lend the same story moment a completely different feeling. The first sentence above probably sounds like the stories we are most used to. Possibly the second one feels more intimate, like we're right there with Mark at the edge of the pool.

You may prefer to use one tense over the other. You may even strongly dislike reading books that employ the alternate option. I know that for me, the present tense can at times feel distracting—more cloying than intimate. (On the other hand, one of my favorite books by a favorite author is written with this approach.)

Though you might not have any intention of switching the tense you've settled on for your narrative, experiment with both to see how it may affect the *experience* offered by your story. It's an experiment that you might as well do when writing a first draft; you may just hit upon the best way to deliver your narrative and save yourself some revision time down the road.

Choose a paragraph from the lightly-revised piece of writing you did for the Core Activity. Rewrite your piece in the alternative tense (if it's in the past tense, use present tense and vice versa). What happens? Other than the tense, did you have to change any of the details? Do you like it? Do you hate it? Does it offer more possibilities, or limit how you're able to express yourself? Does it make you want to keep going to see how the story continues to unfold?

6

DAY SIX: REST

Y OU'VE BEEN DREAMING, WEBBING, planning and drafting your story. Today, you'll simply take a break. I say 'simply', but sometimes disconnecting from your creative work is the hardest task of all.

Tough as it may be, please do it anyway. Stepping away helps create the distance between you and your writing that is necessary for revision. A rest gives you energy and perspective and helps unlock creative possibilities. It gives you a chance to better see the rough edges and the work that still needs to be done. Perhaps less appreciated but just as important—reading your work after a rest also lets you see *what's already working.*

So...

Do something today other than working on your story.

Don't read it.

Don't tweak it.

Don't add to it.

Don't 'cheat' and fuss with your Character Web or your mini storyboard and claim that you're not really writing.

Just put it all away.

It doesn't matter what else you do today. You could even work on another piece of writing. However, in my experience, the more you can truly press the pause button on writing of any kind, the more effective you will be in your revisions. Think of today as recess.

See you tomorrow!

DAY SEVEN: REVISION

R EVISION IS A CREATIVE step where you evaluate, clarify, redefine, and maybe even dramatically redirect your story. It is far different than proofreading where you're on the hunt for typos, sentence structure issues, grammatical and punctuation problems, etc.

For me, revision can take weeks (or months) of work and results in multiple drafts, some bearing little resemblance to earlier ones. If it sounds like a lot of work—it is. But it's *so* very worthwhile. You get to witness your story getting clearer and clearer before your eyes, like a blurry image coming into sharper focus.

For the following exercises, you'll need a copy of the lightly revised 250-word draft you produced doing **Day Five's Core Activity.** *You may want to print off a fresh copy; I'll be asking you to mark it up with highlights, notes, and other alterations in order to polish and refine.*

SIT ON YOUR HANDS

WARMUP

Special Supplies: copy of your Day Five draft.

~

Y OU'VE TAKEN A BREAK from the writing process. You put your lightly-revised first draft away for a rest in order to come back to it today with energy and fresh eyes.

Now take out that draft, sit on your hands, and read it straight through. The 'sit on your hands' image is a dramatization—but do it if it helps! The intention is to avoid marking up your draft with slashes and x's and clever new phrases on this first pass. Don't touch your paper, pen or your keyboard no matter how badly your fingers itch. Just *read*.

Reading while 'sitting on your hands' gives you a chance to get a big picture view of what you've done so far. It's a chance to experience the flow of your language, witness how one scene connects to the next, gauge your story's pacing and timing, and hear the voice that emerges from the narrative. It's a chance to see your story as a *whole*. In my experience, taking time to appreciate the whole—even when it's in the form of a very rough draft—helps me to make more informed decisions when it comes to revising smaller details. Revising feels less like zeroing in on 'items to fix'; instead, I'm clarifying and polishing parts of the same entity so that it all works *better together*.

As you read in this way, you may well become aware of changes you'll need to make to enhance your draft. That's fine—let these impressions seep into your consciousness. You will have plenty of time to act on them! But resist the urge to break from this big picture point of view in order to zero in on what needs fixing. The moment you do, you're dealing with details, and potentially missing a sense of the whole.

As an extra bit of assurance, I've found this to be true—if a change is important enough to make, your story will demand it from you again the next time you read it through.

FIND THE KEEPERS
WARMUP

Special Supplies: copy of your Day Five draft, a highlighter.

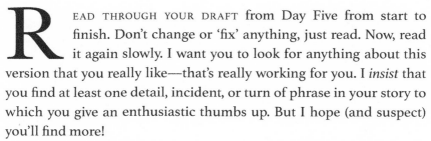

READ THROUGH YOUR DRAFT from Day Five from start to finish. Don't change or 'fix' anything, just read. Now, read it again slowly. I want you to look for anything about this version that you really like—that's really working for you. I *insist* that you find at least one detail, incident, or turn of phrase in your story to which you give an enthusiastic thumbs up. But I hope (and suspect) you'll find more!

If you're working on paper, use a highlighter to illuminate pleasing phrases or sections and/or circle or underline what you love. Use arrows to insert little notes of praise. Of course, you can highlight a digital copy too, or insert comments or notes beside something that really sings.

We often think of revision exclusively as a 'red pen' activity—where you cross things out, make changes and improvements. But I've found that there is value in first acknowledging what you *like*—or even *love*—about your own story. From a 'helpful writer's mindset' point of view, it keeps you connected to your desire to write this story. Practically speaking, by reflecting on what's working, you are learning about your own unique style and about the strengths you can build on as you continue writing and revising.

Finally, we can sometimes get too aggressive with those red pens. In our zeal, we may slash and correct things that actually only need a bit of tweaking. Reading first to 'find the keepers' helps us to take a more balanced approach.

* BIG TO SMALL *
CORE ACTIVITY

Special Supplies: copy of your Day Five draft.

~

R EVISION IS NOT ABOUT proofreading and correcting mistakes; it's about making *creative changes* to your draft. You're focusing on plot, character, and expressive language as opposed to typos, punctuation and mechanics. With this in mind, when it comes to revising a first draft, I like to perform several read-throughs or sweeps, taking a BIG-to-small approach. I identify the big-deal items I'd like to change first, then I read again (and again) for finer changes that should be made.

Let's do a mini revision of your draft from Day Five. You'll read your draft through three times (three 'sweeps') making notes and adjustments to it each time as described below. **The goal is to work toward making a better-than-before second draft.** Don't worry if it's not perfect. (You can read my evolving revisions on the following pages to see what I mean.)

Sweep One—BIG changes first: Read your draft for sense (as in, *'does this make sense?'*). Are there paragraphs or sentences that need to be reordered or removed? Are characters doing or saying things that don't ring true? Does the plot require additional details? Underline and circle text, use arrows to indicate text rearrangements, slash out details that aren't working, make notes in the margin about how you will expand or clarify.

Sweep Two—Smaller changes: Read your draft again. This time as you go, take the time to add in the clarifications you've planned above. You can rewrite or retype your text, or hand-write new text above the old or in the margins with arrows indicating where these changes will go.

Sweep Three—smaller still: Read again, this time for tone and delivery. Can you tweak the language—even a word here and there— to better capture the action, mood or emotion? Make a few such changes.

When you're done, take a little break. When you come back, you can do one more sweep, tweaking until you are satisfied that your draft is a better-than-before, satisfying **second draft**. Use this draft for the **Stretch** activities that follow.

The three most important take-aways from this Core Activity: 1) revision is not the same as proofreading; 2) revising a draft requires multiple read throughs; and 3) expect to write and revise several drafts.

This basic process is just as applicable to a complete draft of a novel as it is to the small writing snippet you are working on now. But I'll include some further thoughts on revising longer manuscripts in the final chapter, 'From Writing Workshop to Writing Your Novel'.

REVISION SWEEP ONE

move? *shows determiniation -more like this!*

Mark shot out of the water at the end of the pool gasping for air. His

splash echoed through the nearly empty space, bouncing off the

high ceiling. The cold light of morning was just breaking through

the floor to ceiling glass on the east side of the pool.

Mark checked the time on his waterproof watch. Not bad. He'd

beaten his best time by a full two seconds. He reset his watch and

prepared to try again. He dug into the water with his powerful

breaststroke.

There was always a moment when Mark would first enter the

water. There was a moment when Mark slipped into the pool at first

when it was too cold, almost like it was telling him to get out, not to

go forward. A shock to the system. But Mark had learned to love

(not great, but something like it...)

that feeling, like waking up on Christmas morning. But when he

pushed off the tile wall and took his first stroke, there was nowhere

or: "he was home."

in the world he'd rather be.   *a true passion? Or an escape?*

He was in the zone now – that first leap into the pool behind him.

Now the sounds of the outside world had fully disappeared, and

everything became muffled. But it wasn't really muffled, it was the

sound of being absolutely alone and focused. Nothing else mattered

but Mark's determined push to be faster, forward.   *Chance for some humor!*

could happen twice, reinformce Mark's dedication

After a few more laps, the lifeguard blows his whistle. The senior

citizens water aerobics class was about to begin. It was time to get

out. Mark pulled himself from the pool, the blast of air somehow

worse than the first plunge, more foreign. The pool was where he

was born to be.

or - could someone in this group
have an impairment - foreshadow
Mark's injury?

REVISION SWEEP TWO
(Incorporates changes from SWEEP ONE)

That first moment Mark slipped into the pool was always too cold. Like the water itself was telling him to get out. But when he pushed off the tile wall and began his first lap, he was home.

Mark shot out of the water at the end of the pool gasping for air. His splash echoed through the nearly empty space, bouncing off the high ceiling. The cold light of morning was just beginning to break through the floor to ceiling glass on the east side of the pool. He checked the time on his waterproof watch. Not bad. He'd beaten his best time by a full two seconds. He reset his watch and prepared to try again. He dug into the water with his powerful breaststroke.

Mark was in the zone now – that first leap into the pool long behind him. The sounds of the outside world had fully disappeared, and everything became muffled. But it wasn't really muffled, it was the sound of being absolutely alone and focused. The lifeguard's sharp whistle penetrated the water. But at that moment, nothing mattered but Mark's determined push to be faster, forward.

Mark propelled himself the last few yards and grasped the pool's edge. He pulled himself up as the lifeguard gave him one last irritated tweet. Mark pulled his goggles up onto the top of his head, pulling at his dark wet hair. He looked up, his eyes meeting the knobby, wrinkled knees of an old man.

"Let's go, Mark! Class is starting," said Brad the lifeguard.

"You can join us," said a laughing old man looking down at Mark. Mark's eyes swooped right to left along a row of withered legs. Walkers and canes lined the wall along with a wheelchair. Senior Citizens AM aerobics.

"No thanks," Mark mumbled, hauling himself from the pool.

*READ ONCE OR TWICE MORE...
...TWEAK UNTIL SATISFIED!*

TAKE A STORY INVENTORY
STRETCH

Special Supplies: Your **revised draft** *from today's Core Activity, a stack of 3 x 5 index cards.*

∾

WHEN YOU'RE REVISING A draft, one of your tasks is to ensure that your plot—the events that make up your story—holds well together. This can mean many different things for different stories. But in general, any writer evaluating plot is asking him/herself questions like: *Is my story clear? Are events staged in the most effective order? Where do I seem too rushed? Where am I dragging? What's missing?*

Revising for plot concerns can involve adding, subtracting, enhancing and reordering scenes, moments and shorter 'beats'. You can certainly add, subtract, enhance and reorder directly within a digital or paper document. But I find it helpful to enlist the help of index cards to conduct a 'story inventory' before changing my draft.

Here's how it works: Grab today's **revised draft** and a stack of 3" x 5" index cards. As you read through your story, summarize each important story moment on one of the cards in a point form note.

(I'm being loose with the term 'story moment' on purpose; let it mean anything that strikes you as worthy of the term.) When you're done, lay the cards out in order on a table or counter (make columns if needed).

Now, read through the cards in order. You might quickly see that you've dwelt too long in a certain part of your story. Try removing a few cards from these places, and reading again to see if your plot still holds together. Maybe your story would be more suspenseful if you hold back certain moments or events until later. Test it out by shuffling some cards around and reading them in their new order. What about that spot where the jump between moments seems forced? Can you brainstorm a few possible 'connector' moments on index cards and fill in the gaps?

Once you have your cards in order, you can turn back to your draft and weave your new ideas into your revisions. *Note that while this technique can help you to refine the shorter story snippet you've been working on during the workshop, it really shines when applied to a longer work like a novel manuscript—so, be sure to try it when you're revising your novel(s)!*

'REVERSE' WEBS

STRETCH

Special Supplies: your **revised draft** *from today's Core Activity, your Character Web (Day Two) and 5 Senses Web (Day Three).*

~

O N DAYS TWO AND three, you used webs to dream and plan story elements. This time, you'll use these same tools to *reflect back to yourself* what you've already written. (You'll be making some new notes and markings on your webs. If you want to keep your 'originals' pristine, consider making copies or snapping a photo.) Here are two optional approaches:

Option #1: Grab your completed **Character Web** and **5 Senses Web** along with a highlighter and a different-colored pen. Re-read your **revised draft**. As you go, highlight any detail on the webs that a reader would learn from reading the draft. Add any new details the draft reveals in the appropriate categories on your webs using the new color (feel free to add categories). You can do this in two reading sweeps—reading once for Character, and a second time for Setting.

Option #2: Make a fresh, blank copy of both web templates. Re-read your **second draft** in two 'sweeps' as above, once for Character details, once for Setting details. On the blank webs, note down anything that someone reading your draft would learn about character or experience in the setting so far in your story.

Using the reverse web method helps you to take stock of what a reader would know, learn or experience when they read your current draft. You can use this information to creatively add or extend missing information as you continue to revise, or to downplay details that didn't come off as you'd hoped (e.g., you imagine your character as bold and direct, but the current dialogue reads makes him sound like an unredeemable jerk).

Of course, not all of the details from your original webs will come across in your small story snippet. In fact, an entire novel manuscript may not end up revealing every single item you planned before plunging into your draft (and that's okay!). Use this technique to assess how well you've expressed the details you want your reader to absorb from this scene or draft iteration.

GET LOUD

STRETCH

Special Supplies: your **revised draft** *from today's Core Activity.*

❧

THE MORE REVISION WORK I do to a project, the more I'm fine-tuning my language. I'm making fewer big-scale changes to the plot and focusing more on getting my wording into shape. I'm working at the best way to express the story that I am experiencing in my own imagination.

Reading my draft out loud to myself is immensely helpful. It helps me to catch overly-wordy sentences that muddy my meaning, spot places where I'm rushing, and notice others where I drag. I think that it also lets me hear my own story the way my readers' inner-narrators will read them.

Find a space and time where you know you'll be uninterrupted and where you'll feel comfortable reading your work out loud to yourself. I personally like to read from a printed off copy with a pencil in hand for noting changes my 'ear' catches (and I like to pace about the room for some reason). But of course, if reading while seated before a screen works for you, that's perfectly fine.

What happens when you try this with your own writing? Do words that made sense on paper (or on your screen) suddenly need tweaking when you read them out loud? Do you notice any quirks in your writing style that you may want to rein in for future drafts?

Reading aloud is also a great tool to use when you're ready to edit and proofread; your ear is a great helper when perfecting the mechanics of your prose.

WRITE YOUR OWN "READER'S REPORT"

STRETCH

*Special Supplies: your **revised draft** from today's Core Activity.*

❧

H ERE'S THE IMAGINARY SCENARIO: your (well-revised!) story draft has made its way to a publishing house. It's now in the hands of a professional reader whose task it is to summarize your story and offer an assessment of its strengths and weaknesses for an editor to review.

For this activity, *you* are the professional reader who will be writing the report.

Your report should be very succinct—no more than one page (it can be single spaced). It should include: a brief summary of the plot, comments on what you perceive as strengths and weaknesses in the plot and/or the writing itself, and any suggestions for improvement. You can write the comments and suggestions in point form or as a bulleted list if you choose. Be sure to use the third person (*The author might consider...*) instead of "I" statements when describing the writing or giving suggestions. The idea here is to gain some objective distance from your draft.

Of course, reporting on your own work is challenging since you are the author—you *know* where this story is going and what you are trying to achieve (even if your current draft isn't a perfect representation just yet). A further challenge today is that you may only be working with a fragment of a story. Don't sweat it. Just try to be as objective as possible. Base your summary and comments on what you *actually see* in the draft before you, as opposed to the story you have in your mind. (So, if this is a slice of your story from somewhere in the middle, don't criticize it for not having a beginning or ending!)

The purpose is to try and see your draft the way it appears to a third party. Gaining this bit of distance may help to shed light on what's working and where you need to revise and offer a sense of what sort of revisions you might attempt.

WRITE THE BACK OF YOUR BOOK
STRETCH

Special Supplies: your **revised draft** *from today's Core Activity.*

~

Y OU'RE GOING TO WRITE 'the back of the book' for your current draft. It's an exercise in summarizing your own work—in getting to the heart of your story. And since text on the back of the book is meant to intrigue readers, this is a great way for you to discover or highlight *for yourself* what intrigues you about your own story.

Turn to **Write the Back of the Book** (Day One: Stretch) for some pointers on how to approach writing this text.

Once you've written the back-of-the-book for your revised draft, compare it one more time to what's actually *in* your second draft. Does your intriguing 'back-of-the-book' text suggest anything to add, emphasize, or clarify in your current story? Does it suggest where you might go next with this tale?

If you did the similar exercise on Day One, compare what you did then to what you produced today.

HOW TO GET FEEDBACK - PART 1
STRETCH

Special Supplies: your **revised draft** *from today's Core Activity, up to four 'feedback friends'.*

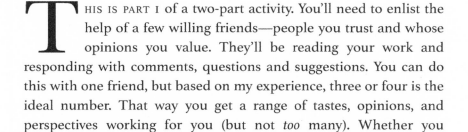

THIS IS PART I of a two-part activity. You'll need to enlist the help of a few willing friends—people you trust and whose opinions you value. They'll be reading your work and responding with comments, questions and suggestions. You can do this with one friend, but based on my experience, three or four is the ideal number. That way you get a range of tastes, opinions, and perspectives working for you (but not *too* many). Whether you approach one reader or several, keep the following in mind:

Tell them what they're looking at. For example, a short story or a snippet from a story (like your workshop draft), a complete first draft of a novel, the first few chapters of your draft novel, etc.

Tell them what you're looking for. Maybe you want to gather general impressions, or their opinion on who they believe to be the intended audience for your story. Maybe you want to know if they think certain plot points are believable. *Tell them what you want to know so you get the answers you need.*

Tell them what you're *not* looking for. For instance, I ask readers of my early drafts *not* to proofread my drafts. I know I'll be making lots of changes, therefore proofreading for spelling, typos and grammar at this stage is a waste of their time and mine.

Agree on how and when the feedback will be delivered. Will you schedule a casual phone chat? Will you communicate through email? Will they insert comments into the body of your text? Make sure that your readers are comfortable with any deadlines set and the method for commenting.

Ask them kindly to provide 'evidence' (a reason) for any comments they share. This doesn't have to be a lengthy process. Just ask them to include a short 'why' with their comments...whether the feedback is positive or of the 'needs-improvement' variety. '*It was good*' is less informative than '*I thought the dialogue between the teenagers rang true*', and so forth.

HOW TO ACT ON FEEDBACK - PART 2
STRETCH

*Special Supplies: your **revised draft** from today's Core Activity and the feedback from your friends after doing the previous activity.*

YOU'VE SHARED YOUR DRAFT with one or more friends. What do you do when the feedback starts rolling in?

First: *remember that feedback is information that will potentially help you to improve your story.* It is *not* the last word on your story's 'worth'—or your worth as a writer.

Second: *listen to and think about ALL the information that comes back to you.* Ask for clarifications or examples if necessary. Enjoy the positive comments; use them as fuel to keep on revising and building on your strengths. Give strong consideration to the comments that challenge or critique your work. They may shed light on a way to vastly improve your story.

Third: *resist the urge to verbally defend your work.* When a feedback reader says something like "I don't understand why Mark would ignore his doctor's advice", it's tempting to list your five very excellent reasons for having written just that. Instead, just say 'all right—I'll think about that'. *And then, think about it.* Maybe your current draft isn't as clear as you thought and there's a way you can improve getting your point and purpose across. On the other hand, maybe your reader just has a different perspective than your own. That doesn't mean she's right and that you need to make a change. *You* are the author, and *you* have the final say. But either way, getting into a debate to validate your current draft—for which *you've* asked for feedback—doesn't get you very far.

Fourth: *be on the lookout for trends.* This is why having more than one reader is valuable. If the same questions, comments and suggestions keep popping up among your feedback crew, that's a pretty good indicator that you should deal with these issues in your revisions. You've also been doing your own reflection on where your draft needs work—how do your readers' comments stack up against your own thoughts?

Fifth: *say thank you!* (In fact, do this first.)

PART III

FROM WRITING WORKSHOP TO WRITING YOUR NOVEL

YOUR NOVEL IS BIGGER than the sample piece of writing you've practiced with this past week. There's going to be 'more' of everything, and not just content: more time drafting, more time revising, and more time resting between steps.

While a novel is a larger work, you can flow through my seven-step method in the same way: *Ideas, Character, Setting, Plot and Planning, Drafting, Rest,* and *Revision*. But there are a few expansions that you might want to consider; things that you can do to build on what you've already practiced to better suit the more expansive story that will be your novel. In the next few pages, I share the specific expansions I have sometimes undertaken for each of my seven steps. You're welcome to try them out, or of course to come up with expansion strategies of your own.

Finally, we'll close out the workshop with one last exercise that will help you to reflect on what you've learned about writing, yourself, and what tools you'll take with you going forward.

EXPANDING ON IDEAS

I F YOU BOUGHT THIS book, you're already contemplating or working with an idea (or maybe several) for a novel. You might be more than ready to skip brainstorming for new Ideas and dive right into work on Character—that's fantastic! But suppose you've finished this workshop and *are* looking to generate a new idea for a novel—or you want to stretch your imagination *as you write*. Here are some possibilities:

- **Revisit any of the Day One Warmup, Core, or Stretch activities.** This time, you're not limited to one day. Give yourself time to really engage your chosen activity or activities. That may mean spending a few hours on a given task or spending many moments over a few weeks doing idea generation exercises.

- **Look again at the story idea you worked with throughout this past week.** Is there something there that could be developed further? Could the character you began to build have a starring role in a more complex adventure? Could the concepts stuck to your mini storyboard be fleshed out with an interesting subplot, or given a sci fi twist and become something utterly intriguing and original? You've spent a week nurturing this concept—it can't hurt to play with some additional possibilities!

- **Take the Write With Your Eyes and Write With Your Ears activities (Day One Warmups) into the real world.** If you did these activities during the workshop, you gathered images and music into your workspace to inspire ideas. You can do the same thing in your day-to-day life. Wherever you go or find yourself, drink in what you see and hear. Wonder about it. Ask yourself 'what if?'. Contemplate your own emotional reactions. You really never know where and when a bit of conversation here, or a gesture there might inspire you.

- **Keep an Ideas Notebook handy.** That way you're always ready to jot down intriguing thoughts, observations and even dreams. I admit, I'm not always diligent about this, but napkins, receipts and my phone have served the same purpose.

EXPANDING ON CHARACTER

I F YOU KNOW YOUR characters well, they can become quite authentic—like living, breathing, thinking, feeling entities. When it comes to writing about them, they may very well start telling you what they would do or say, or what happens next.

When it comes to a novel, you can expand on your Character work in a number of ways:

- **Go beyond your main character.** You spent time with your principal character, but of course you can spend time webbing, writing biographies, sketching, and otherwise developing other important characters who will appear in your novel. As a rule, you'll probably still find that you devote the most time fleshing out your story's hero. (Here's a thought: if you find yourself becoming ever more intrigued with a secondary character and keep turning your energy to their development, ask yourself if perhaps you've picked the wrong hero in the first place. It may be a sign to shift gears and let the character speaking loudest to you to take the lead.)

- **Create more complex webs.** Cover more ground about who your main character is inside and out. Expand the categories. Especially, explore the interior world—the fears, foibles, backstory, skeletons in the closet—to a greater extent.

- **Write fuller character sketches.** Launch from your webs into more detailed written descriptions. Cover any and all details that come to mind and that you believe contribute to the makeup of your characters. And while you may have tried writing biographical or autobiographical overviews, what about a deeper dive into backstory: What watershed moments, family histories, relationships, tragedies, fortunes, etc. have shaped your characters into the people we meet in your story? Write it out.

EXPANDING ON SETTING

WHILE I DO TEND to think of developing Setting as its own separate step, for me it's the aspect of story creation that has the greatest overlap with the others. As I develop my characters, I am already learning more about their world. As I plan my plot, the incidents suggest atmosphere, and grow this setting even further. As I write my draft and my character starts doing things and moving about in his or her world, the setting becomes even more alive.

In addition to spending more creative energy on the activities I've offered for Day Three: Setting, you can expand your work on Setting by going on a **Writer's Walk** (Day One: Stretch). I presented this as an idea generating step, but in truth this is my go-to thinking exercise and my cure-all for creative blocks. At the Setting stage of my writing method, I love to go on long walks and just let the world of my story come into focus in my mind. There's something about moving around in the real world that lures me into my story's world. I encourage you to try it and see what happens.

Depending on the genre you are writing in, or the mechanics of the plot you are planning, the setting/world of your story may require more deliberate and detailed thought. In that case, I recommend that you check out or look again at **Make a Map** and **Write a Brief History of Your World** (both Day Three Stretch activities). Take these strategies and work them up to the level of intricacy required by your novel.

EXPANDING ON PLOT AND PLANNING

T HE MINI STORYBOARD IS a great tool for envisioning your story from start to finish while providing a quick path to the actual drafting of your manuscript. During this work-shop, you may have used it for a smaller-scale story or piece of writing—but it definitely works for envisioning the basic outline of a novel, too.

My **storyboard technique** may be quite enough planning to get you going on your first draft. It may even be the most elaborate plan you've ever tried! If it works for you, please use it and get down to some writing.

On the other hand, you might want to take this plan and expand on it. You're looking for a way to zero in on the intricacies of your plot before you start your draft. Here are some approaches I've taken on some of my projects:

Finesse your mini storyboard.

You used sticky notes for a reason! You can switch things around, add additional notes, take some away, plot the elements of a subplot with another color—even move it all to a larger surface.

Make a bigger board.

Grab a big stack of sticky notes or index cards. In point form, write down *every* event that you think will happen in your story (include the key events from your mini board). If you're imagining a subplot—a parallel story that will dovetail with the main action—write out what happens in it on different-colored cards. Lay your cards on a big table, stick them on a wall, or pin them to a big bulletin board. Keep rearranging, adding and subtracting events until you see a fairly well-developed story blueprint. Snap photos of your board if you can't or don't want to keep putting it away only to lay it all out again.

Write a Story Summary.

Summarize your story from start to finish. You can pretend this is a 'pitch' to an editor. Challenge yourself to limit this written summary to one or two typed pages of text. This forces you to do a better job distilling your thoughts. *What are the main themes? The key events? Who are the most important characters? What is the overall mood, tone and purpose of your story?* A summary that gets to the heart of things may help you to draft with better clarity.

Write a Chapter Synopsis.

Write a brief paragraph describing each potential chapter or section of your book. Think of it as an expansion of your Story Summary (above). This nice, neat sort of summary has helped to get me on track with some of my past drafts.

Remember to Start Writing!

Too much planning can become a form of procrastination. (Trust me—I know!). Planning has its place, but at some point you need to stop 'figuring out your story' and commit to writing it. There's a certain creative alchemy that happens when you write; ideas often spring to life as you shape your narrative in a way that they don't when you're developing a storyboard or synopsis.

Two strategies for preventing 'planning procrastination': 1) Mark a date on the calendar by which you commit to stop planning and start writing, even if you haven't finished your plan; and 2) tell yourself that you can always revisit your plan if you get stuck while writing your draft.

EXPANDING ON DRAFTING

ALTHOUGH THIS IS SUCH an important step, there's really not much more to say about writing your draft besides this: *you need to find a way to do it and keep at it.*

The **500/500 Method** (Day Five: Core) is what works for me. Setting a word count goal that I can attain rain or shine, and then rewarding myself with a bit of light revision—a task I happen to enjoy—has proven successful. Perhaps the best part is how after just a few days, I tend to get into a flow, writing more and more at each sitting—often easily surpassing my 500 word minimum. Even still, I don't increase my target word count; instead I revel in how much I've exceeded it. (A bit of a mind game maybe, but it works!)

I hope you'll give the method a try. But you might find you have a different writing personality. There may be something off-putting to you about my approach. That's okay! When it comes to getting through a draft, it's about setting the kind of schedule or goal that *you* will show up for. Maybe this means increasing your daily word count to something more than 500 words and forgetting about doing any polishing. Possibly a target page count (3 pages a day, five days a week) instead of a word count sounds more like it. Or, perhaps you'd respond to a goal related to time, such as "I will write from 1pm until

4pm on weekdays", or "I will write for one hour each day before leaving for work", or even "I will write fifteen hours a week"—and you find those hours when you can throughout the week. Find the rhythm that works for you—but do try to find a rhythm.

One more point: Who says you need to write Chapter One, then Two, then Three? Maybe you're really stuck somewhere in Chapter Five, but you can vividly picture a critical scene in Chapter Sixteen. By all means, make Chapter Sixteen your day's writing task. You might be imagining a scene but don't have a clue where it will go. Write it and worry about placement later! When you keep at it in this way, you keep up your momentum. Not only will you get through your draft more quickly but you're likely to get back in the flow.

EXPANDING ON REST

I FIRMLY BELIEVE IN the power of resting your work and your writer's self. During this workshop, I asked you to rest for one day. When it comes to writing a draft of your novel, it stands to reason that your resting period should be longer. So, how long?

The answer depends on the writer, and perhaps on the amount of time you've poured into writing your draft. I can't give you an absolute formula, like 'a 50,000 word draft requires a one-week resting period'. The point of a rest is to give yourself perspective—a chance to look at your work with more objectivity so that you can make the changes that you need to make and appreciate what is wonderful and worthy of building upon. I find this to be almost impossible when reading with the bleary eyes of one who finished drafting at midnight the night before.

In my own experience, I've found that anything less than a week is too little resting time. The draft is still too fresh in the mind. For me, even if I've stepped away for the past five days, my brain is still dancing with the dialogue, delighting in descriptions, and committed to the plot decisions I've made. After a week, my creative unconscious calms down enough to let me *begin* to see the cracks and holes and possibly mull over potential creative solutions. Honestly, two weeks off or more is even better for me.

So, the closest I'll come to giving you an absolute timeline for rest is what I've personally found to be true: one week is okay, two is decent, and three weeks (or more) may be even better. Plenty of writers give it far more time than this, so it depends very much on the person and the project.

The other point I'd like to make: until now, I've been talking about taking a break between your first draft and your first revision. The reality is, your revisions may result in new drafts or at least significant changes to a current draft. *Don't forget to also give yourself a rest after you've written a second, third, or fourth draft or made major creative changes.* The resting times between later drafts may be shorter since the story is getting more refined—closer to what your novel will be. Use your judgment, but don't underestimate the power of stepping away in order to come back with more clarity.

EXPANDING ON REVISION

REVISING IS NOT ONLY a lot *like* writing a draft, it *is* writing. You're playing with language. You're clarifying. You're often creating anew. You're shaping your story into what it will ultimately become. Revision is hard work, but not only is it necessary—it's *so* worth it.

I personally enjoy the revision stage most of all. This is not to say I don't find it frustrating and tedious at times. But on a practical level, I feel more hopeful and energized polishing up writing that already exists on the page versus facing the blank page of a new draft. And it really is a self-rewarding process—you get closer to the story you've been dreaming of, and you start to see it with a much clearer focus.

When it comes to revising a draft of your novel, I highly recommend starting your revision period with my **Sit On Your Hands** (Day Seven: Warmup). This means doing a full read-through without making any changes, appreciating what's there, and just letting it all sink in. Then, turn to the **BIG to small** approach that you practiced in Day Seven's Core Activity. You don't want to begin by devoting hours to the minutiae of a single paragraph that you might ultimately slash from your story (although this might still happen on occasion).

I also recommend actively seeking out and incorporating reader feedback as described in the last two Stretch activities on Day Seven (**How to Get Feedback** and **How to Act on Feedback**). Related to this is setting revision deadlines for yourself. Like over-planning before you write, revision can become its own weird form of procrastination. Enlisting feedback friends and setting a deadline by which time you promise to deliver your (revised) draft can help you to get your writing out the door. If you are lucky enough to have very patient friends, ask them if they will read and give feedback on your evolving drafts. It might be wise to budget for a few lunches that you can treat these friends to (and of course this is also what the 'acknowledgments' section of a book is for!).

Remember that you will probably go through the process of revising, redrafting, and revising again a number of times. Take heart—every author does it. And each time it should get a bit easier as your story gets clearer.

SOME LAST THOUGHTS: DON'T BE AFRAID TO ZIG ZAG

S OMETIMES AS A WRITER you *flow*. You may *flow* when it comes to your method, one step followed by the next and then the next— like we did in our workshop week together.

Your writing itself may *flow*. You start your draft at your story's beginning, writing scene after scene in sequence until THE END.

Or, your style and language—the words you are weaving together —feel as though it's coming to you so easily it *flows*.

But other times as a writer, you *zig zag*. You might be working on a character web, but before you're done, you're hit with an inspiration to write a scene. And that scene may not be the first of your story, but an incident somewhere in the middle. Then you're struck with a new idea to pin on your storyboard. Once you've finished zig zagging back to your character web, you feel the need to go for a walk to contemplate your story's world...

My *plan* is certainly to flow through my writing steps in order. But sometimes inspiration arrives at unexpected times. I choose to view these as exciting creative moments instead of disruption. If I'm working on character but have a brilliant, I-can't-forget-this idea for a scene, I'd better zig over to drafting for a bit. I just try to zag on back to where I left off.

On the other hand, sometimes I'm trying to flow—*hoping* to flow!
—but I get stuck. Maybe I get stuck on a writing step, or I find myself
blocked at a tricky juncture in my draft. This is when I deliberately
use zig zagging as a *strategy* to help me get back into the flow. Rather
than banging my head against that writer's block, or abandoning my
writing altogether, I choose to zig zag to another step or to another
scene in my story. I may not be flowing along 'in order', but I've kept
connected to my writing and my rhythm, and I'm much more likely
to find a way back to flowing.

So, I'm here to tell you that zig zagging is okay! A sense of flow
and a state of flow may be what we strive for as writers. It certainly
sounds more orderly than zig zagging around. But you're likely to do
some of both as you write your novel. It's perfectly okay and may
even be the best thing you can do for your writing.

A BRIEF WORKSHOP REFLECTION

MOST WORKSHOPS END WITH time for personal reflection and *The One Week Writing Workshop* is no different. I encourage you to grab your journal and use the questions below to do one last exercise—some helpful musing over what you experienced this past week.

I'd like you to give yourself a chance to think about the things that went well, the things that may have been tricky, and most importantly—*why*. This way, you can go forward with your writing armed with a strong sense of what works for you, and what may not.

- What was your favorite writing activity and why?
- Did this activity prompt you to think in a new way or allow you to play at something you know you already love? Explore this a bit.
- During the workshop, did you expand upon or tweak any activities? In what ways?
- Was there an activity that you disliked or found uncomfortable? Why do you think this was the case? Explore this a bit.

- If the disliked activity was simply not to your taste, what might you do instead when it comes to your own novel writing?
- If the disliked activity helped identify an area where you suspect you want to grow as a writer, list two or three ways that you can get the necessary information or to practice what you believe you need.
- Were there any activities that you didn't try the first time, but that you know you want to try in the future? Which ones?
- Let's assume you'll be using the seven-step method in your future writing. Which specific activities would you include? What other tactics and strategies (your own, from other books, from other learning) might you add? Write out your potential writing plan.

THE BEST REMEDIES FOR _____

E VEN WITH A SOLID method to follow, there are bound to be times when you feel stuck, confused, uninspired or frustrated. Let *The One Week Writing Workshop* help! Below is a quick guide listing common writing 'blocks', and the specific activities I recommend for busting through.

"I Can't Get Started...At All!"

- Re-read the **Icebreakers** section
- Do ANY activity from **DAY ONE**
- **Write With Your Eyes** (Day One: Warmup)
- **Animal Action Words** (Day Five: Stretch)
- READ some great fiction!

"I Can't Get Started Drafting."

- **Start on Page 1, Page 10 or Page 95** (Day Five: Warmup)
- **Beginnings Can Be Choosy** (Day Five: Warmup)

- **Curtains Open** (Day Four). *Create a new Curtains Open idea for your story; write from there!*

"My Character(s) Feels Lifeless!"

- **The Journal Entry** (Day Two: Stretch)—for any of your characters
- **'Reverse' Webs** (Day Seven: Stretch)
- **Take it to the Mirror** (Day Five: Stretch)

"I Don't Know Where to Begin With My Revisions."

- **DAY SIX: REST**—consider extending your 'writing recess'
- **Find the Keepers** (Day Seven: Warmup)—a reminder to build on things you're already doing well.
- **How to Get Feedback** and **How to Act On Feedback** (both Day Seven Stretches)

"My Plot Feels Blah — HELP!"

- **Take a Story Inventory** (Day Seven: Stretch)
- **Game Changers and Best Efforts** (Day Four) — revisit/change your Game Changer on your mini storyboard
- **Dwell Amongst the Books** (Day One: Stretch)

"My Prose Feels Blah — HELP!"

- **More Show, Less Tell** (Day Five: Stretch)
- **Practice Point of View** (Day Five: Stretch)
- **Get Loud** (Day Seven: Stretch)

"I Want to Toss My Notebook/Computer Out the Window!!"

- **The Writer's Walk** (Day One: Stretch)
- **Assemble a Character Scrapbook Page** (Day Two: Stretch)
- **Make a Map** (Day Three: Stretch)
- **Build Your Story's World** (Day Three: Stretch)
- **Step Away and Get Active** (Day One: Stretch)

ACKNOWLEDGMENTS

Thank you to everyone who encouraged me on this project:

For Anita, who not only read multiple drafts but who 'lived the book' and helped inspire much of it during our joint workshop sessions. For Elenore, who read every iteration and enthusiastically tested the activities in order to give me the best feedback possible (though what she really did was dazzle me with her creativity as a writer).

For Marnie, who could see the connections, pathways and possibilities and helped me to make the best of them all. For Jocelyn, whose artistic, creative, and encouraging spirit breathed laughter into my draft and stays with me always.

For my mom who sparked my love of books with 'one chapter a night', and for my dad and our many deep talks about the writer's craft. For Matthew who showed me how two people can write together and encourage each other across the distance. For Allison who was always up for a brainstorming session, and generously shared her wealth of knowledge from the communications field.

For the teachers I learned from and with, and who generously gave me the floor in their classrooms—especially for Lise and Fay and their regular invitations to help grow their writing communities.

For all the brave, daring, creative workshop participants I've worked with, from the writers in the first grade to the young-at-heart.

And especially for Colin, who always believed that *The One Week Writing Workshop* would make a good book.

ABOUT THE AUTHOR

Karin Adams holds a Master of Arts degree from the University of Winnipeg and pursued doctoral studies at Harvard University, focusing on ancient languages and literature. After seven years as a university instructor, she returned to her first love—creative writing. Karin is the author of five middle grade novels including the acclaimed *Frostbite Hotel*. She combines her passions for teaching and writing in her inspiring workshops for writers. Visit her website at **www.karinadams.com.**

Sign up for the online video course of
***The One Week Writing Workshop* at**
www.authorinyourcorner.com

 facebook.com/karin.adams.author

 x.com/karin_adams

instagram.com/karin.adams.author

ALSO BY KARIN ADAMS

Mermaid Warrior Squad

My Best Friend is a Viral Dancing Zombie

Frostbite Hotel

No TV? No Fair!

Lights! Curtains! Cows!

Made in the USA
Coppell, TX
07 December 2024

41935771R00125